T0355369

The Stock Ticker and the Superjumbo

The Stock Ticker and the Superjumbo:

How the Democrats Can Once Again Become America's Dominant Political Party

Rick Perlstein

PRICKLY PARADIGM PRESS
CHICAGO

A *BOSTON REVIEW* BOOK

© *Boston Review* 2005
All rights reserved.

Prickly Paradigm Press, LLC
5629 South University Avenue
Chicago, Il 60637

www.prickly-paradigm.com

ISBN: 0-9761475-0-5
LCCN: 2005921570

Printed in the United States of America on acid-free paper.

Table of Contents

I begin with a parable about politics. Once upon a time, in 1916, William Boeing founded an aircraft company with a single-minded commitment to building the best airplanes the world had ever seen. With America's entry into World War I, the company boomed, then went bust when the war ended. So Bill Boeing converted his factory into a carpentry shop—anything so that he could survive to keep on developing airplanes. That became the Boeing way, the very essence of the company's corporate identity: the willingness to stake itself to the long term for the sake of building something enduring.

Seed capital from big government helped, of course. The technology behind the bombers that Boeing built to help America win World War II would soon contribute to another American triumph: the invention of cheap and readily available passenger air service. Only a week after the B-52 bomber made its maiden flight in 1952, the Boeing board of directors celebrated their success by sinking $16 million into a project to develop a jet-propelled passenger plane. It was a huge gamble. It paid off. With the rise of the 707, Boeing became one of the world's great corporations.

In the 1960s Boeing took an even mightier gamble, setting more than 12,000 engineers to work day and night to turn a failed military transport into the aeronautical equivalent of the Model T—a "jumbo jet" to bring transcontinental flight to the masses. The course was numbingly hazardous. It also appeared foolish, since the market for passenger jets was depressed. At one point during the $2 billion saga the company went 18 months without a single domestic passenger-jet order. The first 747 sold in 1970. That year and the next, the company was forced to lay off 60 percent of its workers to keep the project going. Boeing even considered dropping out of the aviation business altogether. This era was made famous in local history by a billboard reading, "Will the last person to leave Seattle please turn off the lights."

Well. Long story short, Boeing's persistence paid off. In 1978, airlines ordered eighty-three 747s, and Boeing's returns were the highest of the Fortune 500 companies. Boeing made $20 billion over a decade on that original $2 billion investment. Bullheadedness carried the day.

A nice little story, but in order to turn it into a parable, I must introduce our second character, the upstart. In 1967, France, Germany, and the United

Kingdom established a consortium, Airbus, to take on Boeing's de facto monopoly. The strategy was plainly Boeing-esque: Airbus's ownership structure and managerial culture were self-consciously crafted to eschew short-term profit, to patiently cradle a long-term risk. And long-term the risk was: it was eight more years before the company sold a single plane. By the late 1980s the consortium had paid off only $500 million of a $25.8 billion debt. Airbus's member nations had thrown $13 billion from their treasuries down an apparent abyss.

So it is not surprising that in the middle of the 1990s, when an Airbus executive boasted of plans to far surpass Boeing by the year 2003, Boeing's CEO Phil Condit simply laughed imperiously.

Phil Condit was the CEO hired to fix what was seen, in the context of contemporary American capitalism, as a fatal flaw in Boeing's institutional model: its long-term orientation. Wall Street didn't like it. "All stock markets tend to value short-term profits more highly than long-term profits," explains the British commentator Will Hutton in his important book, *A Declaration of Interdependence: Why America Should Join the World*. That was why in the middle of the 1980s, Boeing's stock traded at $7 a share even though the company's net worth was equivalent to $75 a share. In 1987, the Texas corporate raider T. Boone Pickens attempted a hostile takeover of Boeing with the goal of "unlocking" the hidden value buried within: selling off slow-moving divisions, liquidating excess capacity, trimming research and development—turning a dinosaur into a lean, mean, short-term-value-producing machine.

Pickens lost the battle—Boeing fought off his raid—but Wall Street won the war. Boeing began to play by stock-ticker rules. Plans for bigger, better planes were cut back. So were investments in R&D, personnel, and overhead. Condit described the new strategy: "We are going into a value-based environment where unit cost, return on investment, shareholder return are the measures by which you'll be judged."

By 1997—the year Phil Condit was laughing at Airbus—Boeing had become a Wall Street favorite and a powerful force, engineering a hostile takeover of its competitor McDonnell Douglas. By then Airbus had begun the most ambitious civil aviation project in the history of humanity, a "superjumbo" nearly 50 percent larger than the 747 and, it promised, more fuel efficient than a family car. In 1997, Boeing announced that it wouldn't try to compete to build a superjumbo: no more foolish gambles for them. Bill Boeing would have rolled over in his grave, but Wall Street loved it. Boeing's stock price shot up to a record high, $60 a share.

The last laugh, of course, belongs to Airbus. After six more years of carefully shepherding its paleo-capitalistic vision, eschewing short-term gain all the while, Airbus now fills almost 60 percent of new commercial-aircraft orders. The A380 superjumbo has frozen sales of 747s. Boeing has become so desperate to maintain its market position that it engineered a deal to lease 767 jet tankers to the Pentagon—which not only reversed its previous strategy of using Pentagon money as seed capital for advances in civilian aviation but, as Boeing now admits, involved unethical practices. Phil

Condit resigned amid the scandal. That pleased stock-holders: Boeing now trades at a healthy $44 a share.

A company called Boeing will likely hang on for the foreseeable future. But, writes one financial journalist, "the odds are good that Boeing will be out of the commercial aircraft business in ten years."

Is that an unhappy ending? Only if you are a citizen of the United States. According to a report by two University of Buffalo researchers, commercial aviation is "the single most important sector of the U.S. economy in terms of skilled production jobs, value added and exports." And so the political-economy lesson of our parable is plain to see.

But I promised you a parable about politics. So let us bring out the political resonances from the aeronautical shadows.

It was around the time the CEO of Boeing brought on a short-term boost in his company's fortunes by announcing that he was canceling plans to design a superjumbo that the chief executive of a certain political party stepped into the well of the House to announce that he would not be extending his own institution's long-term, risky, carefully stewarded, sometimes even apparently foolhardy grand project. That would be Bill Clinton, declaring that "the age of big government is over" in his 1996 State of the Union Address.

It worked. His stock—his party's stock—shot back up, and he won his reelection even after the historic blow by Newt Gingrich's conservatives, the rival upstarts stewarding their own multigenerational political project.

The New Deal, inaugurated in the 1930s, succeeded in some goals at first and failed in others, but always instilled its vision in the next generation of Democrats. Some parts of the vision—health care for the aged under Social Security—took 30 years to reach fruition. And until the Democrats abandoned universal health care in the 1990s, they'd been trying for almost *60 years*. But after their electoral traumas of the '70s, '80s, and '90s, jettisoning such dinosaurs seemed to be what the market demanded.

We are left with a political party whose fixation on shifts in public opinion is hawk-like, one that concertedly questions core principles in the interests of flexibility. This may have helped in the short term. And certainly, elections in America being winner-take-all propositions, the short term is crucially important. But now that John Kerry has been turned back in the presidential election, now that the Senate favors Republicans 55 seats to 45 and the Republicans have also increased their advantage in the House, the focus must be on rebuilding. But not merely for 2006, or 2008. Winning the next congressional race, and the next presidential race, is not the only problem Democrats face. It is not even their greatest problem. The issue I'm concerned with here is more profound. Too often, Democrats win their immediate battles precisely in a way that hurts them in the long term. They make Boeing's kind of mistake.

How, instead, can Democrats begin winning in a way that puts them back on the road to their former position as the dominant party in the United States?

The year 1977 was the Democrats' most bountiful in terms of a key indicator: party identification. Fifty-one percent of Americans called themselves Democrats. Only 21 percent called themselves Republicans. The postwar numbers before Watergate were not quite as high, but comparable. Now, a just about equal number call themselves Democrats and Republicans. Coincident with this shift was a breathtaking historical reversal: the Republican Party became the party of great dreams, with a long-term project, "conservatism," that Republicans have stuck with even when it seemed foolhardy, even when its individual tenets were demonstrably unpopular.

Why does this matter, as long as the Democrats are still able to win plenty of elections? It matters for a bedrock political-science reason: party identification is the most reliable predictor of whether someone will vote for a given candidate. It is a mighty store of value, party identity, "which we now know is a form of social identity," notes the Democratic pollster Stanley Greenberg, "not unlike ethnicity or race, with considerable durability over time." The Republicans understand this explicitly. Their 2004 presidential strategy was "designed around a plan to increase members of the electorate calling themselves Republicans," according to a November 8, 2004 *Washington Post* article.

The fewer people who identify themselves as Democrats, the harder you have to work—and the greater the cost—to get them to vote Democratic in any particular election. You have to play by stock-ticker rules; you have to cater to their short-term whims.

So when does the Democratic Party end up looking like Boeing—so hollowed out by short-term thinking, so stripped of people proud to identify with it, that it can't compete in the big leagues at all?

* * *

My argument is about what the Democrats have to do to win the elections of 2018. Why 2018? It's an off-year election. Presidential elections are short-term projects. For the Democrats to "win" in 2018, they will need more than a president in the White House: they will need to take back both houses of Congress. They will need to win back the operational control of the government they enjoyed through much of the 20th century. Then they will once again be the dominant party in American politics. They will have won the war. And they will not win the elections of 2018 without winning many elections along the way.

My argument is structural. It's about time horizons, why a long-term time horizon is valuable in itself. We are now embarked on a very, very long march. Some moment-of-truth decisions about what kind of party the Democratic Party is going to be have to be made: the party of the stock ticker, as it is now, or the party of the superjumbo, as it was then. It is time, now, to think big.

And that is the opposite of the message that the consultants associated with the Democratic center have been monotonously driving home for the last 20 years. As Al From and Bruce Reed of the Democratic

Leadership Council put it in a memo in 2004 deriding the rise of Howard Dean, even most Democrats "don't swoon when they hear a candidate say it's time for Democrats to dream again." What is striking is that experts associated with the party's more liberal factions think in similar terms.

Stanley Greenberg is the Democratic pollster whose book, *Middle Class Dreams: The Politics and Power of the New Majority*, is most closely associated with the argument that the Democrats need to focus on the traditional core of their liberalism—economic fairness—in order to prosper electorally. His new treatise, *The Two Americas: Our Current Political Deadlock and How to Break It*, presents the remarkable finding that no less than three quarters of Americans favor a federal mandate "requiring business to offer private health insurance for their employees"—a radical reform by today's policy standards. But what is striking is that in this entire book, Greenberg only makes a few substantive, specific policy prescriptions—and the most prominent is a recommendation for an *individual* health-care mandate, that government should require citizens to buy their own health insurance "much as drivers have responsibility for acquiring auto insurance."

It reminds me of the time Nelson Rockefeller, upon his inauguration as governor of New York in 1959, tried to mandate that every New Yorker spend about $2,000 in today's dollars on a home bomb shelter. He was shocked when his advisers told him how many citizens would balk at what seemed to him such a piddling and crucial expense.

Where does this come from, this astonishing lack of political will that finds liberal pollsters, armed with liberal poll results, thinking with the economic arrogance of billionaires? To begin to understand this, it behooves us to talk about liberalism and the baby boomers.

To start with some matters of definition. This beast we call "liberalism"—in its *genus Americanus*, at least—is a notoriously complicated animal. Its philosophy is rooted in the notion of human beings as autonomous agents. With the realization that formal autonomy meant little without the means to sustain a decent life, its practical definition in this century came to encompass the various kinds of government arrangements democratically devised to share the social burden. What we now mean by the word was summarized with unmatched elegance by Maury Maverick, the Texas congressman who led a caucus in the 1930s that tried to push the New Deal to the left. He called liberalism "freedom plus groceries." As a definition, it cannot be improved upon—although scholars may prefer John Rawls's formulation, that for justice to thrive the minimum worth of liberty must be maximized.

The groceries part, the different ways in which liberals devised to vouchsafe enough material resources for everyone (whatever the divergent conceptions of "enough"), makes for a complex history. I won't get into the technicalities except to note the existence of the commitment as one of liberalism's constants and to observe that such a commitment almost invariably requires a political imagination geared toward the long term.

Now consider the shifting terrain represented by the "freedom" part of Maury Maverick's formulation. In the second half of the 20th century, it expanded considerably: activities once seen as outside the normal purview of civil life came increasingly to be seen by liberals as advances worth struggling over *politically*. At the same time, the battle was joined by conservatives—and, in my own reading, the relationship of conservatism to liberalism is very much a chicken-and-egg kind of thing—politicizing their own, contrary vision of the proper social order.

That's a mouthful. Let me restate it in just three words: the '60s happened. Civil-rights movements pushed boldly to extend the American promise to those previously excluded. Soon, there came a rise in antinomian violence. In the dark recesses of many white voters' minds, such violence, both quasi-political (street riots) and apolitical (street crime), came to seem inextricably linked to those civil-rights movements and to liberalism itself. It was around the same time that many civil-rights activists turned to expressions of ethnic particularism that some liberals were pleased to embrace, though other liberals saw them as betraying liberalism's very core ideals. Meanwhile, new ideas about how, and how aggressively, to deliver the groceries came to the fore. President Johnson promised a War on Poverty, driven by a wizardly new Keynesian confidence that an economy of unprecedented abundance could deliver more groceries to everyone. The surge in expectations led to some aggressive activism on the part of the poor themselves and to a short-lived technical consensus among experts on both the left and the right that a "guaranteed minimum income" was a natural goal toward which both Democratic and Republican policymakers should aspire.

All these developments were not without their backlashes. They came together in 1972 when the Democrats ran a candidate, George McGovern, who was presumed to embody the soul of the new liberalism in all its grandiosity. The candidate of "acid, amnesty, and abortion," as his critics dubbed him, whose main domestic plank was a guaranteed minimum income for all Americans whether they worked or not, whose dashiki-wearing delegates shoved aside old political bosses for representation at the Democratic National Convention, lost in one of the most humiliating landslides in American presidential history. Liberalism had come to seem not a universalist creed, something for all Americans to embrace, but a particularist creed.

The problem that followed from the McGovern campaign was that when people thought about the Democratic Party, the image that came to mind was toxic to Democratic candidates' electoral fortunes, especially in the South and parts of Middle America. The image was of people who burned the flag, of homosexuals and feminists traducing the traditional family, of a reflexive disdain for the projection of American power abroad, of tax-and-spend liberals who lectured Middle America about its moral shortcomings. Most damagingly, the reforms of the 1960s and '70s were interpreted as a payoff to uppity blacks. An extreme form of that perception was expressed by the longtime Democratic Party warhorse Harry McPherson, who told *The Washington Post* after Walter Mondale's 1984 defeat, "Blacks own the Democratic Party. White Protestant male Democrats are an endangered species." A more realistic indictment came from the DLC's Will Marshall. He said of that 1984 election, "It helped convince me that the national Democratic Party drag was such that good candidates were carrying an albatross around their necks with the words 'Democratic Party' written on it when they went in to elections."

It may not be exaggerating to say that all big-league Democratic strategizing ever since has been a series of attempts to overcome this image. Like so many in politics today, most Democratic consultants are still telling stories about the 1960s.

* * *

I often reflect that the modern-day folks who are most hung up on the 1960s are not the baby boomers who followed the Grateful Dead or who still put messages about sticking it to the Man on the bumpers of their microbuses, but the boomers who are consciously or unconsciously obsessed with the idea that they might be accused of once having done these things or of still thinking this way. Among this group are Democratic analysts who present clear evidence that white, middle-class, Middle American voters *no longer harbor these stereotypes themselves* but who draw conclusions *contrary to that data* as if the stereotype were as fresh as this morning's newspaper.*

Stanley Greenberg makes for the most interesting case. It is Greenberg's argument of long standing that the new appeals for rights associated with the '60s social movements were perceived by the white middle and working classes as a costly intrusion on their own prerogatives. Costly to them literally—and here I quote Kevin Phillips from *The Emerging Republican Majority*—because "the Democratic Party fell victim to the ideological impetus of a liberalism which had carried it beyond programs taxing the few for the benefit of the many...to programs taxing the many on behalf of the few." But also costly figuratively, costly psychologically, because the new social lassitude associated with liberalism affronted cherished values.

In its worst incarnation this backlash was frankly racist, but it has always been Greenberg's special contribution to remind us that even the most racially motivated grass-roots retreat from liberalism was never a retreat from liberalism *tout court*. "The white steelworkers in Alabama and the white mineworkers in South Africa," he wrote in the preface to *The Two Americas*, "whatever their awful role in excluding blacks, were not without social democratic impulses."

---

*The immediate response to Kerry's defeat emphasized a related interpretation that voters rejected the Democrats because of a revulsion for post-'60s libertinism, voting for George Bush on the issue of "moral values." This early assessment was not borne out by later analysis of the exit poll data, which indicates that Bush performed no better in 2004 among heavy churchgoers or rural voters than he had in 2000—but that most of his gains came among voters making more than $100,000. See http://poly-sigh.blogspot.com/2004/11/morals-vs-class.html

Thus the basic policy prescription of the School of Greenberg. Over the last 50 years, according to Greenberg, the divisions between Democrats and Republicans "have become increasingly cultural, crowding out other important issues for the country." Thomas Byrne Edsall and Mary Edsall's *Chain Reaction: The Impact of Race, Rights, and Taxes on American Politics* describes the result: "Conservatism...capitalized on these conflicts with growing sophistication." People who once were Democrats for economic reasons now voted for Republicans for cultural reasons. The conclusion: Democrats should stick to economic populism and distance themselves from the kinds of freedom associated with the 1960s.

But the School of Greenberg's economic populism, it is important to note, was of an explicitly limited sort. This is another legacy of the 1960s. Back in liberalism's mid-century heyday Democrats repeated a maxim about why their big-government programs were a political natural and the Republicans' limited-government nostrums a political nonstarter: "Nobody shoots Santa Claus." But in the wake of the stagflation of the 1970s, as John Judis and Ruy Teixeira observe in *The Emerging Democratic Majority*, "A growing number of Americans had come to believe that government intervention"—associated with Johnson-era economic liberalism—was the cause. "In September 1973 only 32 percent of Americans agreed that 'the best government is the government that governs the least'; by February 1981, 59 percent agreed."

The upshot: stick to delivering the groceries. Just do it in small, measured doses.

The Democratic Leadership Council takes the same critique further. It says, more or less, that delivering groceries (what they call "outcomes") is illegitimate—that Democrats should focus on giving people the opportunity to get the groceries for themselves. Of course, liberals like Greenberg embrace the same abstraction. But in practice, the followers of the DLC pressure the government to do much less.

Central to the present DLC strategy for saving the party is a focus on "wired workers" as the key swing voters the Democrats must win in order to prosper. They "are optimistic about their economic prospects," writes the DLC pollster Mark Penn,

> and they favor a small, nonbureaucratic form of government activism that equips people to help themselves.... Outdated appeals to class grievances and attacks upon corporate perfidy only alienate [these] new constituencies and ring increasingly hollow.

It's easy to take cheap shots at the DLC's expense, but in fact it's perfectly reasonable to suppose that postindustrial "knowledge workers" hold great potential for the Democratic coalition. But not for the reason the DLC supposes—just the opposite. One of Ruy Teixeira and John Judis's most important points in *The Emerging Democratic Majority* is that the white-collar workers the Census Bureau classifies as "professionals," as opposed to "managers," used to form the most reliably Republican voting bloc, but they have gone for the Democrats 52 to 40 percent over the last four elections. One reason: "they have had their autonomy undercut by corporate and institutional managers who have introduced work rules, overseen their output, controlled the prices they charge and the incomes they receive." In a word, they have been proletarianized—proud craftspeople increasingly falling pray to "alien market standards of performance that conflict with their own standards of excellence." (One remarkable index of this shift is the American Medical Association, once the most conservative major professional guild in America and the only one to endorse Barry Goldwater. In the first half of 2001, 67 percent of their contributions went to Democrats.)

But then Judis and Teixeira introduce a baby boomer kind of hang-up into their analysis.

The main argument of their book is that the increasing numbers of such voters make an eventual Democratic majority a near inevitability. But when they talk about what kind of political vision Democrats need in order to reach them, they assert, without adducing evidence, that these voters are *skeptical* of "the government's supplanting and repealing the operation of the market." These voters "want incremental, careful reforms that will substantially increase healthcare coverage and perhaps universalize it, but not a large, new bureaucracy that will replace the entire private healthcare market." They believe the most important role of government is to "equip Americans with the tools to be effective workers in a high-tech society, but they don't want government to guarantee everyone a job through public spending."

Now maybe the members of Judis and Teixeira's emerging Democratic majority indeed think in pretty much the same way as do Mark Penn's "wired workers," and maybe to veer toward economic populism is to risk losing their support. But might not it also be likely—especially with fears about the outsourcing of professional jobs abroad being the hottest new political issue—that the reason these people are becoming Democrats is *despite* the party's turn from market interventionism, not because of it?

When its intellectuals are ready simply to *presume* the validity of a theory that may in fact be the *opposite* of the truth, it's no wonder the Democratic Party has become so timid.

* * *

When social scientists render conclusions at odds with their own data, it is reasonable to wonder why. Again, one reason may be generational. Dissenters who *do* call for a bolder Democratic Party—one thinks of Robert Borosage of the Campaign for America's Future—are sometimes dismissed as throwbacks to the '60s. Well, I can't be dismissed as a throwback. The '60s ended when I was less than three months old. The traumas that shaped the world view of a Teixeira, a Greenberg, a Judis were the post-'60s backfirings of left-of-center boldness. The same goes for Al From, whose formative political experience, he has told me, was McGovern's loss in 1972. The traumas of my own political generation, conversely, were the backfirings of left-of-center *timidity*.

Which may be why, when I read these writers' stories about the history of the past 25 years, I don't know what they're talking about.

When Al From sent out the memo to potential members announcing the formation of the Democratic Leadership Council in 1985 he blamed the Democrats' decline on "consistent pursuit of wrongheaded, losing strategies" such as Walter Mondale's "making blatant appeals to liberal and minority interest groups in the hopes of building a winning coalition where a majority, under normal circumstances, simply does not exist." As a historian, I looked up the record. And what I learned was that Walter Mondale's grand strategy for his general election campaign was a promise to cut the deficit by two thirds in his first term through $92 billion of spending cuts and a tax hike. He also promised $30 billion in spending to restore some of Ronald Reagan's cuts in social services—the money coming from other cuts elsewhere. On the stump to blue-collar workers, Mondale would lecture on the "misalignment of currency."

Now I'm not sure what kind of strategy it would have taken to beat Ronald Reagan's "Morning in America" in 1984. But this was surely not it. Deficit reduction was also not a direct appeal to liberal and minority interest groups.

Cut to 1988 and the Dukakis campaign, the inspiration for the famous 1989 DLC monograph by William Galston and Elaine Kamarck, *The Politics of*

Evasion: Democrats and the Presidency, which argued that the Democrats had degenerated into "liberal fundamentalism." But the closer I studied the actual content of that campaign, the more I trusted the assessment of Sidney Blumenthal in his book on the 1988 election, *Pledging Allegiance*: "Dukakis's very inability to offer any definition of liberalism was taken as perhaps his most encouraging trait" by Democrats that year, he writes. "It was seen as an enormous shrewdness, a form of wisdom. Dukakis's politics of lowered expectations, his career of slashing budgets and tax cuts, made him seem a new kind of Democrat, a man of his time."

Thus, under the slogan "This election is not about ideology, it's about competence," did Dukakis, incompetently, run. I'll buy anyone a steak dinner who can, without a trip online or to the library, come up with a single "liberal fundamentalist" program that Dukakis advocated that year. That Dukakis retreated from liberalism in reality is not to say that the Republicans didn't succeed in *labeling* him as liberal—an important distinction. The Republicans will attempt this in every election, whether the candidate is liberal or not.

And what about Bill Clinton in 1992? I once interviewed a liberal political activist who explained to me that the DLC loses every election but always manages to win the battle to interpret every election. It's an exaggeration with more than a grain of truth. "Bill Clinton would not have been able to win the election if he had not run as a New Democrat, addressing the problems of cultural breakdown, the perceived practical failures of government, and public doubts about the welfare state," the New Democrat historian and loyalist Kenneth Baer writes. As for cultural breakdown, any American who read a newspaper in 1992 knew that Bill Clinton had tried marijuana, violated the sanctity of his marriage vows, and dodged the draft. They voted for him anyway. And anyone who heard Bill Clinton speak during the 1992 general election season knows that a constant refrain was a promise of $50 billion a year in new investments in cities and $50 billion a year in new funding for education—and, what's more, a first hundred days to rival FDR's, culminating in the passage of a plan to deliver health care to every American. He also, of course, made noises about his toughness on crime, his commitment to beat down government bloat, his (vague) pledge to "end welfare as we know it." He made rhetorical flourishes about issues like school choice. But the argument that DLC talking points won him the election cannot be sustained. It would also be wrong to argue that nobody-shoots-Santa-Claus-style liberalism did it. It was Ross Perot who won the election for Clinton, taking away many votes that ordinarily would have gone to Bush. Bush, with the economy as it was, had the lowest approval rating of any president seeking reelection in history. My little mutt Buster could have beaten George H.W. Bush in 1992.

* * *

Revisionism might seem a knottier course as our story progresses. Wasn't it Clinton's turn to a paleoliberal plan for universal health care that slew the Democrats in the 1994 Congressional elections, his neoliberalism that allowed him to get, as the subtitle of Dick Morris's memoir *Behind the Oval Office* puts it, "Reelected Against All Odds"?

But isn't it also logical to hypothesize that the Democrats lost Congress not for proposing health care, but for *losing* on health care?

A suggestive piece of evidence comes from Greenberg, who had his focus groups write imaginary postcards to President Bush and his Democratic opponent. The most poignant comes from a Florida swing voter, who wrote, plaintively: "Dear Democratic Nominee, What can you actually do better. [sic.] What happened to the health care programs you promised us 8 years ago?"

The point is supported by an argument of the political scientist Martin Wattenberg, who has demonstrated that "registered nonvoters in 1994 were consistently more pro-Democratic than were voters on a variety of measures of partisanship." This suggests that the real triumph of the Republicans in 1994 was not ginning up any kind of new national consensus on their issues, but in motivating their own core voters to create a temporary mirage of such a consensus. And thus, when the Republican congress tried to legislate, radically, based on this purblind "mandate," the more massive electorate in the presidential year 1996, more reflective of the ideological predilections of registered voters as a whole, found the Republican Senate leader Bob Dole easy to reject. "Whereas the credit for Clinton's comeback in 1996 is often given to the triangulation strategy designed by his pollster Dick Morris," Wattenberg concludes, "these results suggest that another plausible factor was the increase in turnout from 1994 to 1996."

Let me clear the decks, and let me do it bluntly. There is a more elegant explanation for why the Democrats succeeded in every election of the 1990s but one. It is, simply, that the core Democratic message of economic populism appeals to people—despite, not because of, the Democrats' retreat from that selfsame message. And that the old '60s bugaboos no longer keep people from voting for Democrats because so many voters are too young to remember, or care.

Look at the data on the white, working-class counties of the industrial north that at mid-century were once so reliably Democratic but whose Wallace-Nixon-Goldwater Democrat turn so traumatized liberal confidence by the 1980s. Jefferson, just south of St. Louis, went 57 percent Democratic in 1960, 42.6 percent in 1968, 38.6 percent in 1972, and 36.71 percent in 1984. Macomb, north of Detroit: 63 percent for JFK, 66 percent for Ronald Reagan in 1984. Ninety percent of former Reagan-Democrat counties returned to the Democrats for Clinton's first presidential run. They voted around the national median in 2000 (slightly for Gore), with Republican gains in 2004 well below Bush's gains elsewhere (1.7 percent in Macomb, compared to three percent nationwide). The idea that counties in the industrial midwest where white, blue collar ethnics congregate are particular danger spots for the Democrats is dead and deserves to be buried.

Now, to point this out is to give the DLC some ground: this is testament to Clinton's success in making the Democratic Party worthy of these people's trust again. But I'd like to call a witness on my behalf. His name is...Bill Clinton. "The more they believe that you're careful with tax money and responsible in the way you run the programs and require responsibility from citizens," the former president told *The American Prospect* in an important interview last fall, "the more the public in general is willing to be liberal in the expenditure of tax money.... The Democrats ought to all pocket some of the gains I made." To believe deep down that white, blue-collar voters might somehow slip back into an atavistic pining for George Wallace is to insult these voters and traduce Bill Clinton's accomplishment. The Democrats need to start trusting that their 1990s gains were real, and that people vote for Democrats because they're attracted to economic populism, not repelled by it.

Another place where Democrats need to start trusting these gains is in the realm of foreign policy. Recent failures in Iraq point out just how threadbare the old stereotypes about wimpy Democrats and muscular Republicans remain. In polls, people still claim to trust the Republicans over the Democrats to keep them safe. But the numbers are becoming softer all the time. After the disasters of the 2002 off-year elections, Bill Clinton lamented in an address to the DLC, "When people feel uncertain, they'd rather have somebody who's strong and wrong than somebody who's weak and right." Here is an example in which the Democrat who can't trust that Bill Clinton's gains were real is Bill Clinton. George W. Bush has been serving Democrats a future campaign issue on a platter: that an appearance of strength, when rooted in incompetence, strategic blindness, and ideological obsession, is weakness. If Democrats can't convert the distrust produced by George Bush's numbskull unilateralism into a trust in Democrats on this issue, perhaps they don't deserve to win elections.

I understand why it might be hard for baby-boomer Democrats to shed the sense that they have to look a little more like the Republican Party in order to restore voters' trust: getting spurned by Reagan Democrats was the shock that defined their political lives. Bill Clinton is an outstanding example of this reaction: from his gubernatorial loss in Arkansas in 1980, he learned to be cautious about pushing liberalism forever after. Same for Joe Lieberman, Indiana Senator Evan Bayh (now DLC chairman)—who watched his father get strangled by Ronald Reagan's coattails—and Stanley Greenberg, who, holding focus groups in Macomb County, Michigan, in 1985, found voters raging that "blacks constitute the explanation for their vulnerability and for almost everything that has gone wrong in their lives" and that the Democratic Party was in thrall to them. No wonder he's careful not to offend those same folks now.

But Greenberg presents no evidence in his latest book that any of that vituperation remains. Instead, when Greenberg asks voters to describe the Democratic Party, he doesn't get back a description of the party of hippies, welfare queens, and gays; he gets a description of the party of...nothing at all:

"I think they lost their focus," says one informant. "I think they are a little disorganized right now," answers another.

"They need leadership."

"On the sidelines."

"Fumbling."

"Confused."

"Losing."

"Scared."

Which brings us back to the question of stock tickers and superjumbos. Who wants to identify with an unfocused, disorganized, leaderless, sidelined, fumbling, confused, losing, scared organization? Vote with it sometimes, maybe, but identify with it? No one I know. Even if that institution happens to offer more of what people say they want. If people don't know what you stand for, they won't identify with you. Change your message to try to win each passing election, and soon you may start losing them all.

So what's the alternative? What should the Democrats' consistent, long-term message consist of? I will avoid prescribing what it should be, other than to note that for reasons of history and structure it must tend to the work of economic equality. There are really two reasons to stay away from details. First, they would distract from the real point of this essay, which is not about programs but about structure. Second, there are lots of possibilities for programs, and it would be misleading to focus on some favored set. It could be universal single-payer health care. It could be free college education or universal pre-kindergarten or both. It could be a program to make the government

the employer of last resort, putting the underem-
ployed to work rebuilding infrastructure. It is not the
work of a day, a month, or even a year to settle on
what the course should be. I argue here only that
there must be a course.

Why must these programs tend to the work of
economic equality? One reason is structural (or "path-
dependent," as the social scientists say): the modern
Democratic Party's strongest store of cultural identity,
of value built over time—its "brand identity," as the
marketers put it—is in its work producing economic
equality. Abandoning it makes as much sense as
McDonald's deciding to drop the hamburgers and
remake itself into a chain of pancake houses.

Another reason is more simple—numbskull
simple. Any marketing executive will tell you that you
can't build a brand out of stuff the people say they
don't want. And what do Americans say they want?
According to the pollsters, exactly what the
Democratic Party was once famous for giving them:
economic populism.

* * *

In *The Two Americas* Greenberg presents a fascinating
chart that records his subjects' rankings of our country's problems. It reads like the score for an Old
Democrat symphony. Of the top eight concerns, only
one, by the traditional reckoning, helps the
Republicans: "Rogue nations, like Iran and North
Korea, armed with weapons of mass destruction and
working together with global terrorist organizations."

It's ranked in second place, designated "extremely serious" or "very serious" by 72 percent of respondents.
But before that, in first place, is the biggest problem:
"the state of health care in America," a major concern
for 77 percent. Four through eight read thus: "two-
parent families spending 22 or fewer hours with their
children every week in order to work and earn
enough"; "the state of education in America"; "the
middle class being squeezed, because their incomes are
stagnant while prices are skyrocketing for housing,
college tuition, and health care, with employers
contributing less each year"; "big corporations having
too much influence"; and "the growing inequality of
income in America." (The issue in third place, "rapidly
rising federal deficits," represents a tactical disadvantage for the Bush administration.)

All these are rated major problems by 52
percent or more. When you get near the bottom of
the list, you start getting Republican issues: "out-of-
control government spending and programs";
"outdated government regulations"; and "the high
taxes on businesses and individuals."

That would be the crown jewel of the
Republican agenda, which only 15 percent rate an
"extremely serious problem" and 15 percent call "very
serious." All three of the above are worried over by
less than 45 percent of respondents.

Greenberg asks a group of voters what they
think about "big corporations":

They spit out, "money," "greed," and "Enron."
They "try and run the little guy out" and "have too

much control over the little people." ... "They want more and more and more.... "It really makes me question and just lose faith in everything that we are supposed to believe in."

It is a topic, he concludes, that one of his focus-group subsets approaches "with revulsion formerly reserved for Hollywood." These people do not come from one of his swing-voter subsets. They are "Country Folks," rural men and women without a college education, a demographic that went for Bush over Gore almost two to one.

It's a story you find again and again, buried in his pages. Fifty-two percent of elderly non-college-educated men call themselves Republicans, only 39 percent Democrats—and only 37 percent of them believe that regulation does more harm than good. As for his national sample as a whole, "a 55 percent majority favors a larger government effort to reduce the differences between high- and middle-income people. The majority reaches 65 percent to aggressively shut down corporate loopholes and shelters.... More than 60 percent of Americans say CEO wrong-doing is a 'widespread problem' in a system that is failing"—a figure "well in excess of the percent getting 'very angry' about the federal government spending the social security surplus, as a modest point of comparison."

From this, Greenberg makes an extraordinary admission: the anticorporate reaction is not the strongest among the Democratic loyalists; it is not a "base strategy" in conventional political terms. "The anticorporate appeal reaches into the contested world, and even the Republican loyalist world."

So why aren't these people Democrats?

* * *

I suspect that in part it has to do with the fact that responding to these concerns would require a commitment to economic liberalism, which means a commitment to the kind of time horizon that Democrats, so fixated on the two-year election cycle, don't even know how to think about. If you can't see beyond the two-year election cycle, you certainly can't be thinking about a commitment as serious as "a larger government effort to reduce the differences between high- and middle-income people." That simply takes a while—in the conception, in the execution, and, not least, in the political promotion. Instead—to take a notorious Dick Morris idea that made it into Clinton's 1996 State of the Union Address—the voters get the federal promotion of school uniforms.

It's not that any Democrat ever sits down and says, I only care about what happens in the next two years. The sentiment has been displaced. It is expressed every time a Democrat fetishizes the problem of reaching "swing voters" above all else.

Those who vote neither habitually for Democrats nor habitually for Republicans are, of course, important voters: there are many of them, more of them all the time, and without a sizable number of them, neither party would win any pluralities.

But what, structurally, is a swing voter? We return to the example of Boeing. Swing voters are like short-term stockholders. They are attracted to one position or another because of what's in it for them at any particular moment. When that position no longer pays, it is abandoned.

Try to woo a bloc of swing voters—"security moms," "NASCAR dads," whatever—who are by definition fickle, and a political party hollows itself out by ignoring stakeholders who aren't short-term: activists, institutions like labor, minorities whose commitment to the Democratic Party is historic.

By this theory, the analogue to T. Boone Pickens or "Chainsaw Al" Dunlop is...Dick Morris.*

Bill Clinton hired Dick Morris to prevent what was seen, in the context of a single career, as an unacceptable horror: a looming reelection loss. Morris persuaded him that the modern Democratic Party's founding principle—long-term investment in programs to create more economic equality—was

---

*To belabor the comparison but to broaden the social critique, in this analogy a bloc of swing voters resembles an institutional investor. The rise of these massive blocks of capital, controlled by pension and mutual funds, has precisely because of their aggregated power come to drive corporate decision-making. And institutional investors, Will Hutton notes, on average "turn over 40 percent of their portfolio in a year, looking for higher returns." Back in the time when a company like Boeing could thrive, in 1960, "Wall Street turned over only 12 percent of its entire capitalization." It is a source of the cult of the short-term in American capitalism. The irony is that though the development of a majority "investor class" has been treated as a democratizing force in capitalism, it is the opposite. Pension- and mutual-fund holders' money is invested by cartels, cartels that have weakened the voice of individual investors; the style of corporate management these cartels demand, by systematically ignoring stakeholders other than shareholders, weaken citizens' other stakes in the economy—their stake, for example, as members of a "working class."

unacceptably inflexible. For Clinton and Morris, the solution was plain. The Democratic Party had to shed everything that was slow-moving and lumbering in its ideological presentation. They had to turn a dinosaur into a lean, mean short-term vote-producing machine.

The Congressional losses of 1994 touched Clinton's deepest anxieties, and made him willing to weaken the institution that made him, for personal survival. Dick Morris did it the way a corporate raider would. By showing indifference to any stakeholder but the swing voter, he gladly risked the loyalty of those who had been willing to stick with the institution through thick and thin. "The fact that it would anger Democrats was not a drawback but a bonus," Stephanopoulos recalls of Morris's strategy—just as angering long-term stakeholders is a bonus for a manager looking to prove to Wall Street his macho *bona fides*. It gives the stock a goose. The only risk being, of course, the long-term health of the institution.

Political scientists, having established that party identification is the best predictor of voting behavior, need to study how many party identifiers the Democrats lost specifically as a result of this kind of thinking. They need to measure the opportunity cost of doing what Dick Morris said needed to be done to win the 1996 election and the opportunity cost of the Morris-like habits that currently saturate Bill Clinton's party. Now that Dick Morris has been disgraced, it's easy to laugh at him. But we all know what happens to those who laugh imperiously in parables. He lost the battle. But did his legacy of stock-ticker thinking also lose Democrats the war?

*   *   *

Some of the evidence is close at hand. It's hard to identify with a party when you don't know what it stands for or how it differs from its opponent. According to exit polls taken during the 2002 congressional elections, only 34 percent of voters thought the two parties differed on the one issue the Democratic leaders Dick Gephardt and Tom Daschle made the core of the congressional campaigns: providing prescription drugs under Medicare. Meanwhile, on another issue of widespread voter concern—the economy, encompassing both the recent corporate scandals and mounting unemployment—the leadership offered no coherent ideas at all. So it was that voters who rated the economy their most important issue voted Republican in House elections 52 percent to 48 percent at a time when the president presiding over the faltering economy was a Republican.

I have noted that many voters no longer remember the Democratic Party's reputation as the institutional embodiment of the worst excesses of the 1960s. But there's something else they don't remember: that the Democrats were once the clear and obvious institutional embodiment of their own economic interests.

How do we know this? Judis and Teixeira make a fascinating observation about the increasing number of voters who refuse to identify with a party:

"When the new independent vote is broken down, it reveals a trend towards the Democrats in the 1990s and a clear and substantial Democratic partisan advantage.... Once these independents are assigned the party they are closer to, Democrats enjoy a 13 percent advantage over Republicans." They add that among the 15 most independent-rich states, ten belong to the Democrats— big ones like Connecticut, Illinois, Michigan, and Virginia. Two of them swing. The other three are tiny.

Here's a riddle: what is a swing voter? More and more, it is an American who thinks like a Democrat but refuses to identify as one.

As President Clinton put it in the *American Prospect* interview, "The public is operationally progressive and rhetorically conservative." And if it is true that party identification—which, as Greenberg argues, is a form of social identity that endures over the long term—is the best predictor of voter behavior, isn't getting this selfsame public to identify with the Democratic Party much, much more than half the solution?

* * *

So how to do it? Democrats must stop looking leaderless, fumbling, unfocused, disorganized, and confused. They must give voters something to identify with. They must no longer judge themselves sophisticated when they cancel all the old long-term dreams. They need new long-term dreams.

Ronald Reagan used to say that there are no easy answers but there are simple answers. The answer to this problem is simple, and not easy. The Democrats need to make commitments, or a network of commitments, that do not waver from election to election. If you are trying to build an institution that commands respect and power unto generations—that can reproduce itself—wise superjumbo projects have intrinsic value, whatever their precise content, whether they end up failing or succeeding. The investments pay off, not in immediate profit, but in the equity that comes from sweat. Because they require patience, they build fortitude. Because they require their stakeholders to take risks, they inspire an evangelical commitment to redeeming the risk. Even if they don't succeed, they leave something behind: an institutional infrastructure, a rich network of stakeholders at multiple levels of commitment and intensity—an institutional soul.

Think about this mystery: why, if so many of their individual issues poll abysmally—demonstrated in the Greenberg data cited above—have the Republicans been able to pull even with the Democrats in voter identification and win back operational control of the U.S. government?

The right wing of the Republican Party after World War II had a theory: the reason the Democrats were the dominant political force was the Republican establishment's stock-ticker-like devotion to whatever happened to be the political fashion of the moment— its self-conscious embrace of swing voters. (Conservatives called the Republican establishment's ideology the "dime-store New Deal": the Democrats' ideas, only cheaper.)

The conservatives' original willingness to stake themselves to the long term was reflected in gallows humor: "I think we had better pull in our belts and buckle down to a long period of real impotence. Hell, the catacombs were good enough for the Christians," the publisher of the *National Review*, William Rusher, joked in 1960. When they finally got their moment in the sun, nominating one of their own for the presidency in 1964 by hook and by crook, the results were so disastrous that Richard Rovere of *The New Yorker*, voicing the consensus view, proclaimed, "the election has finished the Goldwater school of political reaction."

They would, of course, eventually be vindicated. Conservatism went bust, conservatives made some adjustments—anything to keep on building conservatism. That became the conservative way, the very essence of its political charter: a willingness to stake itself to the long term. Progress was steady. In 1966 a bunch of new conservative governors and congressmen were voted in. In 1980 Americans elected one of them, Ronald Reagan, as their president. In 1994 Republicans achieved what a previous generation would have deemed impossible: control of Congress. And in 1995 Bill Clinton paid Reagan tribute by adopting many of his political positions, which had also been Barry Goldwater's positions.

What had happened in the interim, and why? Obviously, an enormously complex and contingent history unfolded, too complex to do justice to here.

But one reason for their success was formal. It was their longer time horizon. They built the brand. They made sure everyone knew what it meant to be a

Republican. And this very willingness to commit
became the margin of difference that allowed a set of
not all that popular ideas to become a winning platform.*

Shortly before Halloween of 2003, a very self-
satisfied Newt Gingrich gave an interview to Susan
Stamberg on the subject of power. She asked him if he
missed the perquisites of being Speaker of the House.
He answered,

> If you're trying to do big things, petty power isn't
> very interesting; it doesn't really matter very much,

---

*Among liberals, another theory for the Republicans' success has become
dominant. It is that the Republicans have mastered the dark art of political
fear-mongering, a tactic beneath the Democrats. The "fear" argument is
absurd, bathetic, and self-congratulatory. Presidential politics has always
been an arena of fear, a dark continent. Conveying a political vision is
almost always like telling a bedtime story: the voters' fears must be named,
described, to convince them that this particular candidate is the one to
vanquish the scary monster under the bed—that this candidate, not the
opponent, is the guarantor of security. The title of Greenberg's recent op-
ed, "Fly High Above the Battlefield," is an emblem of the problem: flying
above the battlefield has never won Democrats presidential elections (with
the possible, extraordinary exception of Jimmy Carter in 1976). Instead, it
has lost them elections (certainly Adlai Stevenson in 1952 and 1956 and
Dukakis in 1988). Greenberg believes in a message he calls the "JFK
Opportunity Democrats." Presented with studied vagueness, it is an appeal
to sunny optimism and high-minded consensualism. Beyond the oddity of
embracing as a model a campaign that basically produced a tie, I wonder
where the idea comes from that Jack Kennedy's political style was especially high-minded, his message one of sunny optimism. His most celebrated moment as a campaigner, the first debate against Richard Nixon,
was a scary litany of Soviet advances. His central domestic campaign
plank, Medicare, was sold through images of Grandmother dying sick and
alone. As president, much of the time he was on TV he was warning
America that the world might soon end. No, "fear" is not the secret to the
Republicans' success—unless you are referring to the Democrats' timidity
in the kind of fear-naming that is a natural and legitimate part of any
successful political campaign.

if you're trying to do something historic...
Remember that I spent from 1978 to 1994—that's
16 years—to create a majority. So I'm comfortable
with long-term projects.... I kind of measure things
different [than most]."

The Democrats need to start making these
kinds of measurements: to dream some political and
policy dreams that are big enough to take 16 years or
more to build.

Conservative political ideas are bad, and they
have been winning. Liberal political ideas are good,
and they can win. But this final message is for all of
you who might have been nodding along with the essay
the whole time, smiling in agreement: you shouldn't
have been, at least not if you were following all my
points. For this argument is for the objective necessity
of political risk for irreversible commitments. And irreversible commitments are not anything to smile glibly
at. If risk is not frightening, it is nothing at all.
Republicans began their march to an irreversible
commitment to the full conservative program in 1964.
It led that year to an atrocious defeat. I'm not saying
the Democrats need to embrace an economic liberalism superjumbo, and then lose, in order to win. I'm
saying that they must embrace an economic liberalism
superjumbo, and they must stick with it even if they
lose, in order to win big. Dream again, or die.

Still Thinking Big

William A. Galston

Rick Perlstein's essay is such a complex mixture of
insight, misinterpretation, and outright error that I
hardly know where to begin. Like Perlstein, I believe
that a political party must stand for something that
matters and must seek to rally a sustainable majority
around its core beliefs. Like Perlstein, I believe that
chasing short-term political profits is likely to lead to
the erosion of brand loyalty. And for the record: Dick
Morris is not a New Democrat. He is not an Old
Democrat. Based on his list of clients, I doubt that he
is a Democrat at all. He is a man of some tactical
shrewdness and no discernible principles. Like most

other DLCers, I deplored his prominence in the 1996 Clinton campaign, in part in the belief that it would reinforce the canard that the New Democrat movement was nothing more than a congeries of unprincipled tactics. Perlstein's piece bears out my fears.

I agree with Perlstein that the problems facing the Democratic Party today are more than cosmetic. The beginning of wisdom is to recognize that the Democratic Party has lost the structural advantage it inherited from the New Deal and must now compete with Republicans at best on equal terms. I cannot tell for certain why Perlstein thinks that happened. Here is my thumbnail sketch.

Nixon's rout of McGovern need not have signaled the end of the Democrats' national majority. But by 1980, three large events had generated tectonic shifts in the electorate. Runaway inflation ended economic recovery and eroded real incomes while forcing tens of millions of Americans into the upper tax brackets. The Carter administration's schizophrenic foreign policy, culminating in its shocked response to the Soviet invasion of Afghanistan, weakened the public's confidence in Democrats' stewardship of foreign policy. And President Carter failed to redeem the promissory note he had issued to evangelical Protestants during the 1976 campaign, dooming Democrats' prospects in the South and setting into motion the long-term realignment of the electorate around religious and cultural issues.

Walter Mondale's defeat in 1984 tells us very little: with 5.8 percent real economic growth and no major foreign entanglements, I doubt that a

Democratic ticket headed by Jesus Christ, with Moses as his running mate, would have gotten more than 45 percent of the vote against Reagan-Bush. (Full disclosure: I was Mondale's issues director during that campaign, so the reader is free to discount my judgment.) The fate of the 1988 Democratic standard-bearer is far more revealing. Surely Perlstein remembers the tank ride that crystallized doubts about Michael Dukakis's credibility as commander-in-chief. And surely he remembers the controversies over prison furloughs, the death penalty, and the ACLU that stamped Dukakis as a cultural liberal out of touch with the middle of the electorate.

In the wake of the 1988 fiasco, in which Dukakis turned a 17-point lead into a 7-point defeat, a number of us reached a judgment that I would still endorse today: that the 1970s and 1980s had solidified an impression of the Democratic Party as inattentive to the public's economic concerns, out of touch with its cultural beliefs, and unable to defend America's interests abroad. We believed that if the Democrats' 1992 nominee wanted to get a fair hearing for a progressive economic message, which we all endorsed, he would have to address these concerns. That is what Bill Clinton did. Contrary to Perlstein's claim, Clinton's pledge to end welfare as we know it was more than a vague throwaway; it was at the core of Clinton's successful effort to persuade moderate voters that he was a "different kind of Democrat." It is no accident that the campaign featured a TV ad on welfare reform in every swing state during the ten days before the election. That is a contemporaneous fact, not retrospective DLC spin. And by the way, welfare reform was not a political tactic. We proposed it because we believed in it. So did Bill Clinton. And as events proved, we were more right than wrong to do so, and our critics were more wrong than right.

We come now to the beginning of the Clinton administration. Bill Clinton did three big things during his first year in office. He proposed, and drove through a reluctant Congress, a budget plan that laid the foundation for the rapid economic growth of the 1990s, the fruits of which were more broadly shared than at any time in 30 years. Over the opposition of his own party, he pushed successfully for enactment of an ambitious free-trade agenda. And to redeem Harry Truman's 1948 pledge, he proposed a system of universal health care. He did all these things not because he judged that they were popular (at least two of them were not), but because he believed they were right. Perlstein may well be correct that Democrats lost the Congress not for proposing health care, but for losing on it. That leads to the much-debated question of why they lost. I believe that if Democrats had enjoyed a political tailwind rather than a headwind— that is, if the public had been confident rather than skeptical about the effectiveness of government programs—the proposal would have been structured differently and its fate would have been happier. But that is an argument for another day.

The argument that cannot wait concerns the meaning and motivation of the New Democratic movement. In brief: far from abandoning the traditional values and goals of the Democratic Party, we sought to renovate them to meet changing conditions. Let me give one example, drawn from many others. Along with all Democrats, we believed that the working poor were getting a raw deal. But we did not agree that an increase in the minimum wage was the best or only way of improving their condition. Instead, we advocated a massive increase in the Earned Income Tax Credit. Included in Clinton's 1993 budget, it produced a huge income transfer to the working poor. (And, by the way, it was funded through a progressive income-tax increase on the wealthiest two percent of Americans.)

New Democrats spent the years from 1989 through 1992 crafting new policies that we hoped would both promote the common good and spur the long-term resurgence of the Democratic Party. These proposals were gathered in *Mandate for Change*, a densely argued and footnoted 388-page book that repays reading even today. We may have been right; we may have been wrong. But we were not cynical, we were not tactical, and we were not thinking short-term. Rick Perlstein's saga of shell-shocked boomers recklessly pitching their principles overboard makes for engaging reading, but it is a fantasy.

So what are we to make of the 2004 election? No doubt Perlstein will interpret it as confirmation of his thesis. The evidence, however, suggests a different conclusion. The events of September 11 returned defense and foreign policy issues to a level of political salience not seen since 1988. Senator Kerry's ambivalence about the war in Iraq reinforced public doubts about his resolve to prosecute the war on Islamist terrorism with the vigor and determination that people thought appropriate. In this context, the perception of Kerry as a cultural elitist out of touch with the moral sentiments of mainstream America all but sealed his fate.

In short, John Kerry lost the election for much the same reasons that Michael Dukakis lost to George W. Bush's father. Between now and the next election, therefore, Democrats must do what they did after 1988—namely, adjust their agenda and update their policies to meet new challenges. In carrying out this task, New Democrats are part of the solution and not, as Perlstein seems to believe, the heart of the problem.

A Lost Cause

Adolph Reed, Jr.

Rick Perlstein addresses a question that has vexed many left-of-center Democrats since the triumph of Reaganism. Why does the Democratic Party persist in a national political strategy that seems to play into the Republicans' hands?

Perlstein's diagnosis is clever and persuasive, as far as it goes. That elite Democratic discourse remains haunted by Vietnam-era debates meaningless to increasingly large numbers of Americans is interesting and plausible. It seems to me that much of the New Democrat sensibility—especially as articulated by the Clintonistas—has been shaped, at least rhetorically, by specters of "the excesses of McGovernism" or the supposed error of 1968, when Hubert Humphrey's commitment to continuing the war led many on the left to boycott the presidential election. This unhappy nostalgia culminated in the insane fear in 1996—expressed from the Baby Boomer in Chief himself down to Mayor Richard M. Daley—that the Democratic convention in Chicago might become a replay of the debacle of 1968. Perhaps as a metaphor for the Clinton presidency, the DNC and the Daley administration responded preemptively by squashing free speech and freedom of assembly inside and outside the convention and marginalizing left protestors in a small, tightly guarded "protest pen."

It is equally plausible that elite Democratic strategists have become myopic, lurching from election to election, trying to engineer a message that might successfully appeal to each season's magical, mythical swing constituencies. This fetish no doubt reflects a retreat from a politics based on popular mobilization and is bound with increased dependence on inside-the-beltway political consultants.

Perlstein's explanations match the experience of those of us who have complained about the Democrats' ineptitude in national politics, their acceptance of the Republicans' view of the American electorate and its concerns, and their willingness to permit the Republicans to define the terms of political debate—both the range of acceptable positions on the key issues and even the key issues themselves.

From this perspective, continued adherence to a failing strategy looks rather like the institutional equivalent of a mental disorder. It may succeed in a given election, as with Clinton in 1992 (though with the asterisk of Ross Perot's help) and 1996, but occasional success only masks the more fundamental dysfunction. Perlstein describes eloquently why this syndrome is destined to fail.

In principle his proposals for how the Democrats could break out of this cycle and recapture the initiative in political debate are sound and reasonable. Yet his argument raises a question: if we assume that elite Democratic strategists are not mentally ill and are at least as intelligent as we are, why have they clung to their inadequate approach? Why haven't they come on their own to perspectives and proposals like Perlstein's, which are lucid and sensible, if not obvious?

Consultants don't much care, of course: they get paid win or lose, and they have a product to sell—which in this case is partly the idea that their services are a better alternative to political mobilization. To that extent the apt medical analogy may be iatrogenic disease. Not only does pursuit of a technicist, consultant-driven strategy beget electoral failure; each failure becomes evidence for the need to depend even more on the presumptions of the failed strategy. Nevertheless, incumbent officeholders, candidates, and aspirants are pragmatic to a fault, and their main concern is with winning elections. After nearly two decades, it's not likely that they continue to follow this course mainly out of habit, ignorance, or misjudgment. We must assume that their strategy is the product of rational calculation based on the same knowledge we have.

It's not the DLC point of view that needs explaining. Its response to every election cycle, win or lose, is a commitment to the proposition that the party should move farther to the right. Proponents of the DLC's strategy are not primarily misguided, misinformed, or made purblind by an ideology whose strictures they can't throw off. The DLC is a faction within the national Democratic Party that functions like the Club for Growth within the GOP, that is, a self-consciously organized element whose mission is less to restore the Democratic Party as a force in national politics than to reshape it as the Republican Party lite, essentially disfranchising everyone except the investor class. But what of the other Democrats who could be in a position to alter the party's direction? Why can't they break with what my son characterizes as a "Me too, but not so much" response to the GOP's program?

I think the problem is that the national Democratic Party is torn between two constituencies whose interests are fundamentally incompatible. And, no, this doesn't concern race.

Mobilizing the kind of popular electoral base necessary to take back political initiative would require that the Democrats, as Perlstein argues, propound a compelling alternate vision of what public policy should look like and how the country would be governed if it were governed to reflect the interests and concerns of the vast majority of people who live here. That would require sharply differentiating themselves from the Republicans on class grounds. It would require mobilizing around issues such as real national health insurance (eliminating the travesty of corporate health care), restoring and strengthening workers' rights, providing access to high-quality education through college for all, or renegotiating NAFTA and the WTO trade and investment agreements to assert some controls over disinvestment.

The Democrats can't make that kind of appeal because they're no less beholden to corporate and Wall Street interests than the Republicans are. Perlstein's proposals are fine, but they'll fall on deaf ears. The Democrats will by and large continue to cater to those interests and palliate the rest of us with rhetoric. Already they've become the party of fiscal responsibility. Both parties are fundamentally committed to paving the transition to a social regime that is the equivalent of a modern enclosure movement—one that subordinates public functions to the market (including the idea of public good itself), drastically reduces social wage protections, and enforces a draconian social policy. The Democrats favor a more gradual transition, with softer rhetoric than Republican zealots. And that difference isn't always trivial. A Kerry presidency no doubt would have done less irrevocable harm than we can expect with another four years of Bush. But as Kerry tied himself to the "me too, but not so much" approach, the tensions inherent in the Democrats' message made it more difficult than it should have been for him to win.

As we look past Kerry's defeat, though, it's most important to try to mobilize popular support around realizable policy objectives that can speak broadly to people's needs and concerns—and their real fears and anxieties. That's how we can best attempt to shift the terms of political debate, with or without the Democratic Party. Puzzling over how to take back the party from corporate and financial interests and political consultants seems a bit like trying to reform the Catholic Church's homophobia. Our time would be better spent articulating the contours of the world we want and fighting for it. Meanwhile, we can expect the Democratic Party to melt down under the weight of its own contradictions, like the Whigs in the 1850s. The really interesting and exciting questions concern the alternatives that might replace it or emerge from its ashes.

Reality Check

Ruy Teixeira

To put it mildly, I don't agree with Perlstein's essay. Indeed, I hardly know where to start disagreeing.

But start I must. So let's consider the question of party identification. Contrary to what Perlstein says, the Democrats today continue to enjoy an advantage on party ID roughly equal to their average advantage in the period since 1984. Republicans closed the gap in party ID briefly after 9/11, when Bush's popularity surged, but things are now back to normal. Data that show the gap being eliminated generally include that abnormal period and prove nothing other than the well-known political-science finding that when a president's popularity spikes, there is movement in party ID toward the president's party.

I mentioned "the period since 1984." But let's dwell on 1984 itself a bit, since what happened then is important to understanding where Perlstein's analysis goes awry. In 1984, of course, Ronald Reagan obliterated Walter Mondale in the presidential race, receiving 59 percent of the popular vote and winning every state but Minnesota (he also lost in the District of Columbia). In so doing, he won 65 percent of white working voters, carrying this group—formerly the heart of the New Deal coalition—by a stunning 30 points. Moreover, 1984 is the year political scientists generally view as the break point in Democrats' party-ID advantage; before 1984, it was very large, surpassing 20 points in most years; after that it was much smaller, generally in the low- to mid-teens or even the single digits. In fact, if you compare the 1964–1982 period to the 1984–2002 period, their advantage is cut almost precisely in half.

Clearly this election was a debacle of immense proportions for the Democrats. What happened? The best way to think about it is that it was the culmination of a process that had been unfolding since the late 1960s. One part of the process was driven by white opposition to civil rights and, more broadly, white opposition to various programs associated with blacks, including welfare, busing, and affirmative action. Another part of the process was driven by Democrats' association with the stagflation—combined inflation and unemployment with slow economic growth—of the late 1970s. Stagflation fed resentments about race (about high taxes for welfare, which was assumed to go primarily to minorities, and about affirmative action) even as it sowed doubts about Democrats' ability to manage the economy and made the causes that Republicans and business interests proposed for stagflation (government regulation, high taxes, and spending) more plausible.

A third part of the process was driven by a perception of Democratic weakness on foreign policy and standing up to the Soviet Union; the late 1970s saw Soviet-allied regimes take power in Angola, Ethiopia, Yemen, and Nicaragua, and almost get there in El Salvador—not to mention the Iran hostage crisis. Just as many Americans believed Carter and the Democrats had become incapable of managing the economy, they also began to doubt their ability to represent America in the world. The final part of the process was driven by Democrats' association with the counterculture of the '60s, including feminism, gay rights, abortion rights, decriminalization of drugs, and sexual freedom.

That multi-pronged process was what produced 1984, where, as described above, a stunning collapse in white, working-class support for Democrats was matched by a sharp decline in the Democrats' party-ID advantage. Oddly, Perlstein does note some of the changes described above and acknowledges that they hurt the Democrats. But when it comes to the 1984 election, he chooses to focus on Mondale's deficit reduction and tax hike promises as proof that he did not run on a particularly liberal platform that would have reinforced these image problems and therefore suggests that his loss can't be attributed to the Democrats' negative image. He makes much the same claim about Dukakis's losing campaign in 1988; he didn't really run as a liberal, so the Democrats' negative image couldn't have been what killed him.

But choosing not to run as George McGovern did is not the same thing as actually repairing the Democrats' image, and this was what both the Mondale and Dukakis campaigns failed to do. And it is what Bill Clinton, to a significant extent, did manage to do in the 1990s. His two election victories, in which he managed not only to win Democrats' emerging constituencies, such as women, professionals, and minorities, by healthy margins but also carried white, working-class voters (albeit by a single point), were testaments to his success. I certainly agree with Perlstein that his populist approach, particularly in 1992, was part of his success, but so was his New Democrat approach to mending many of the image problems sketched above. Focusing on one without the other won't do; Clinton's success depended on a synthesis of the two approaches. As for Perlstein's claim that his dog Buster could have beaten George H.W. Bush in 1992, I will let this unusually silly—but revealing—observation slide by without further comment.

Perlstein's focus on the populist side of Bill Clinton without giving due credit to the New Democrat side shows he does not understand the depth of the political problems Clinton needed to deal with and that Democrats still have to deal with today.

This is still a country where there is serious concern about the effectiveness of government spending, serious resistance to taxes even for worthy causes, serious concern about Democrats' foreign policy toughness, and serious worries about Democrats' association with non-mainstream social values. Democrats cannot overcome these problems simply by wishing them away (let's not worry about winning, says Perlstein, let's focus on...2018).

The good news is that Democrats are gradually overcoming these problems. They are making good progress on eliminating Democratic defections to the Republican Party (a huge problem in the 1980s) and winning over political independents (who voted Republican in the 1980s but are now leaning Democratic). Building up the Democratic party-ID advantage is a longer-range project, but I believe progress can be made here too (though I am doubtful, for various reasons, that Democrats will be able to regain their pre-1984 advantage in full). But doing so depends on combining the Clinton synthesis Perlstein disdains with some of the broad, large-scale thinking he so clearly favors. But since he did not take such a nuanced approach, his call for large-scale thinking winds up seeming impractical rather than inspirational. As someone who shares his interest in big ideas and long-range strategizing, I think that's a shame.

DIY Politics

Dan Carol

Rick Perlstein's focus on 2018 is spot-on. Because really the only thing we want to mimic about right-wingers' success is their long-term view.

Much—too much, really—has been written that documents how conservative strategists and funders turned things around after the Goldwater defeat. But on our side I think it is important to understand where we have come from—and why—before tackling the challenges we need to get right, as we write the winning script for 2018.

Explaining the "how-did-we-get-into-this-mess" issue need not take very long—I can name that tune in four notes. We got into this mess because we needed to create political leadership opportunities and replace the smoke-filled room with the open-source, collaborative politics that is our future. It's important to remember that if you were a female or an African-American in 1964, there was nowhere to go if you wanted to advance yourself in the Democratic Party or the union movement. So we saw an important and necessary flowering of single-issue movements (civil rights, women's environment, gay and lesbian, and so on) and leadership opportunities. Is this Democratic Party or this Democratic coalition now less than the sum of its parts? You betcha. Were these changes necessary? Of course.

So that was then. And now, how are we going to put Humpty Dumpty—the Democratic coalition—back together again?

First of all, we need to understand that it's not the Democratic Party's problem alone. Legal changes, created by the 2002 McCain-Feingold campaign-finance law, actually make it illegal for the Democratic National Committee to create the coordinated plans for winning presidential states—and of course, that's how we make a president.

So we're going to have to do it all by ourselves by using existing coalitions, new creativity, and a bottom-up, grass-roots organizing model that blends high-tech and high-touch approaches. Essentially, we must quit the habit of blaming "the Democrats" and learn the new skills of "pick up a hammer" politics.

Confused? Think of it this way: every four years there are about 50 million Democratic voters who get counted, more or less, depending on Florida's mood. The rest of the time, the Democratic coalition divides into card-carrying party activists, passionate environmentalists, pro-choice voters, trade-union members, and at least 27 more great flavors of Baskin-Robbins–Democratic–green–progressive–liberal you-name-its. Of course, we're all individuals, we all hate being labeled (so no letters about this!), and we all want more community and more cooperation.

So how can we rally our troops, state by state? Frankly, it's an open question and there is no one-size-fits-all solution. I agree completely with Rick Perlstein that we need to think big and offer optimistic visions, and I have been a proud partner in one such project, the Apollo Alliance, which wants to spend big and use nationalistic instincts to drive a smarter regional economic-investment agenda.

But to re-glue together the Democratic coalition, we're not going to succeed overnight with one big slogan. We really need to think more like Barry Diller and less like FDR—or Boeing. Diller's Internet empire and business model strings together many powerful brand names, but they are all tied together by a common, back-end infrastructure.

In Oregon, for example, where I now live, it may take an army of angry parents to step up and demand serious action to preserve and enhance public education—rather than more bickering over Band-Aid solutions. Doing that right may require organizing every living room, school, place of worship, work-place, and mall into a new network that Salem cannot ignore. It certainly will require "strange bedfellows" politics—since we'll want business leaders to join in and say we need a well-educated work force if Oregon is to incubate new ideas, technologies, and jobs. This new movement will probably also have to take positions on issues besides education—by painting a new vision of Oregon's future. Long-term success may also involve creative "Civics 101" efforts to make clear to voters that sidewalks and fire trucks are not free.

What will this new network be called? Well, it probably won't just be called the Democratic Party. Because it can't involve just Democrats. It probably won't live under any one roof. But this emerging network will end up serving as a focal point for growing new community leaders and inspiring a return to old-fashioned, face-to-face conversations about our future.

In other states, the focal point for organizing new hybrid Democratic networks might involve expanding health care, ending special-interest corporate welfare, investing in green growth, or some other rallying cry that ties together neighbors and communities across the state.

For many political folks used to simpler times, the substitution of loose-knit, state networks for the ease of shopping at "Window A" at the DNC is a sad day. Mixing back together all 31-plus flavors of Democrats into a new, tastier milkshake will take a while as we figure out what messages and values actually engage our voters.

Perlstein's quotation from Will Marshall has it half right: it isn't that the Democratic Party alone is an albatross—any political party would be. So yes, we will want to keep the Democratic brand name while we test-market what sells, and hopefully inspires, political action, affinity, and community-based connections that last.

Yet while a new era is dawning, it need not be dark. State networks, not national parties, will be the easiest place to gain traction and drive social change. So let's dream big and see what works. Let's pursue and repeat the marketing lab experiments that work, while we build a new Democratic Party. If we can finish before 2018, all the better. I'm getting tired.

Fusion Politics

Daniel Cantor

I agree with just about everything Perlstein says. How could any sane progressive think otherwise? We wanted the Democrats to win in '04, even as we knew they would disappoint us in '05. The operative question for me is this: what are the organizational moves needed for the long-term approach he describes to become real? How do we structurally yank Democrats, Republicans, and the entire political discourse to the left?

My suggestion: revive progressive fusion politics. I am talking here about third-party politics in the populist tradition, familiar today to New Yorkers but largely unknown to everyone else. I know of no more powerful tool for forcing Democrats (and even Republicans) in the direction Perlstein wants them to go than the approach of the Working Families Party (WFP) of New York State.

How it works in theory. Fusion is simple. It refers to the electoral tactic of two parties "fusing" on one candidate, meaning the candidate appears twice on the ballot under two separate party labels. "Vote Perlstein for State Assembly," we might say in New York, "but vote for him on the WFP line and send him a message about...health care [or taxes, or living wages, or whatever else the WFP chapter in his district thinks important]." Election Day rolls around, and Rick gets 45 percent as a Democrat, his Republican opponent gets 47 percent, and the last 8 percent shows up on the WFP line. The votes are tallied separately but then added together, and Rick wins 53 percent to 47 percent. But he owes us 8 percent of his victory, and if we continue to organize year-round, he will feel obliged to deliver as best he can on our issues in the legislature, which should in turn help us to get still more votes the next time around.

Fundamentally, fusion is the peculiar, American form of proportional representation, in that it allows political minorities—understood arithmetically—to show their strength and to make coalitions with other parties.

How it works in practice. Since the formation of the WFP in 1998, we have backed some 1,400 candidates on our line. Most were Democrats, a few were

Republicans, and a few were stand-alone WFP candidates who competed with the two major parties when neither major-party candidate appealed to our membership.

About half of our nominees have won. Results on our line vary from race to race and county to county, but it is fair to say that the party has been on a steady upward trajectory. Last November, some 15 percent of the vote in the New York City Council races came in on our line. And the WFP has been the margin of victory for candidates in Suffolk, Albany, Duchess, Monroe, and Westchester counties.

The aim of all this electoral work is not just to win elections but to change policy. Indeed, because we are typically not running our own candidates, we have a huge incentive to do precisely what Perlstein recommends—that is, lead with values like fairness and equality, and issues like living-wage jobs, fair taxes, and educational equity—and in so doing change the very terms of debate. "Vote your Values," says much of our campaign literature, and we believe our values are not only right but popular.

Inside vs. outside. The two contending strategies of the electoral left, in caricature, might be described as the "inside" strategy and the "outside" strategy. The insiders argue for taking over the Democratic Party, which is a fine idea, but they have failed to note that the Democratic Party often takes over you. And the outsiders, most famously the Greens, argue that the whole thing is too rotten and should be avoided. But the outsiders don't actually wish to wield state power, and thus are not relevant for this discussion.

The fusion strategy is an inside–outside approach and gets you, to my way of thinking, the best of both worlds.

Here are four elements of party life that are worth considering:

1. Relationships with elected officials. Every single candidate and elected official wants all the ballot lines he or she can get. That means they are very, very accessible to us.

2. Internal trust and discipline. It is very common for important affiliates of the WFP—there are 85—to lose a vote on a given endorsement. Happens all the time. But nobody leaves, because we have that ballot line, there is always a next election, and no one wants to give up the chance that they might win the next time. Over the last five years, a culture of trust and discipline has developed, the value of which is more or less impossible to overstate. Electoral coalitions inside the Democratic Party are much easier to form, but they also fall apart more easily. A party is harder to build, but much more durable.

3. A home for activists. The WFP chapter meetings around New York are very different than Democratic Party meetings. They are not full of people who are angling for jobs. They are not full of political staffers. They are full of union members, ACORN members, schoolteachers, retirees, tenants, students, immigrants, and anyone else who shares our values. It is very valuable to have an organizational home for such people that is

not the Democratic Party, because it just feels better to them. Our aim is not to end our relationship with the Democratic Party but to change it for the better. And to do that, well, it is good to have a party of one's own.

4. A home for voters. A party is valuable because it allows regular voters who never want to come to meetings to show their allegiance. Pulling the WFP lever is a way for thousands of New Yorkers to signal their aspirations and values. There are about 150,000 people in the state who have the "habit" of voting WFP, and of course we plan to increase that number. As we do, though, it is worth noting that we do not know specifically who most of these people are. And that's fine. We are glad that they look to the WFP for information on which candidates are the best, and thrilled that they want to help us keep officials accountable by increasing our share of the vote.

One Not So Minor Problem. Of course, fusion voting is not legal in most parts of America, but that's not my fault. In the states where it remains legal (Connecticut, Delaware, Mississippi, New York, South Carolina, and South Dakota), we are looking for allies who want to start using it. And we have begun an Expansion Project to look into the possibility of changing the laws in some states via ballot measures, legislative campaigns, or even state-based lawsuits.

So this approach is not for the faint of heart. But think back to the story of Goldwater and the rise of the right that Rick Perlstein told in his wonderful book (*Before the Storm: Barry Goldwater and the*

Unmaking of the American Consensus). These folks had patience. We need to have some too. (They didn't have much irony, but maybe cash is the right-wing substitute.)

Who likes us and who doesn't. The clearest evidence of how the WFP fits in with the world view Perlstein describes is that we are disliked by the center-right of the Democratic Party—people who think the way to win elections is to articulate policy goals about one degree to the left of the Republicans. These folks' bumper sticker should read, "We're more or less like the Republicans, just not as mean."

Who likes us, of course, are the progressive Democrats. They understand that we strengthen the left flank of the Democratic Party by our very existence, just as the Conservative Party in the state has strengthened right-wing Republicans.

A true story, not even a parable, of my own. Five or six years ago, when we first started, we had a phone canvass, which involved calling people at dinnertime and hassling them for money. One of our callers routinely had absurdly long conversations with people and almost never raised any money. Finally I asked someone, what was up with this guy? They said he was terrific, really interested in understanding political change, and needed the job so he could continue work on some hyper-ambitious biography of Barry Goldwater that he claimed to be writing.

It sounded unlikely to me, but anyone who is willing to hit the phones, or hit the doors, gets my respect. The ideology that we need to reverse course and save the country is not so mysterious. What's needed is the will and the organizational structures to keep us energized and honest. I offer fusion politics as one tool that might help, and urge others to explore it.

Movement Politics

Robert B. Reich

I largely agree with Rick Perlstein's argument about the need to focus Democratic energies on building voter support for the long term. My own sense is that we need to put more weight than Perlstein does on the importance of building a movement rather than an organization to which people are loyal. But rather than quarreling with what he says, I will present my own view and leave it to readers to decide whether the differences are subtle or substantial.

Right-wing conservatives are largely in control of America. They run the White House and Congress, and soon, likely, the Supreme Court. Most state governorships and legislatures are also in the hands of Republicans, which gives them power to draw the lines of future congressional districts and thereby keep hold of Congress. Right-wing conservatives now claim most of America's airwaves, in full command of "talk radio" and "yell television." They run most Washington "think tanks." They inhabit some of the most influential positions on Wall Street and in American corporate boardrooms. Radical conservatives are, in short, America's new governing elite.

A little over a decade ago, it looked as if Bill Clinton's "New Democrats" were in firm control. Although Clinton was elected with only a plurality of votes (Ross Perot ran as an independent third-party candidate, taking votes away from the first George Bush), once in office Clinton appeared to enhance his standing as a "new kind of Democrat" by eschewing stands associated with the traditional left. He signed the North American Free Trade Agreement, embraced "fiscal austerity" and deficit reduction, and called for an end to the dole. It seemed as if a new Democratic era had begun. Democrats controlled both houses of Congress. The country seemed solidly behind us. (I say "us" because I was Clinton's Secretary of Labor.)

But within two years, Clinton's ambitious health-care plan was defeated. In the fall of 1994, Republicans took over Congress. Clinton was reelected in 1996, but his second term was mired in scandal, and the country appeared to veer to the right. In 2000, with the country enjoying unparalleled prosperity, George Bush won the presidency (although Al Gore just barely won the popular vote). What happened?

We failed because we failed to build a political movement behind us. America's newly ascendant radical conservatives do have such a movement, which explains a large part of their success. They have developed dedicated sources of money and legions of ground troops who not only get out the vote but also spend the time between elections persuading others to join their ranks. They have devised frames of reference that are used repeatedly in policy debates (among them: it's your money, tax and spend, political correctness, class warfare). They have a system for recruiting and electing officials nationwide who share the same world view and who will vote accordingly. And they have a coherent ideology uniting evangelical Christians, blue-collar whites in the South and West, and big business—an ideology in which foreign enemies, domestic poverty and crime, and homosexuality all must be met with strict punishment and religious orthodoxy.

Democrats have built no analogous movement. Instead, every four years party loyalists throw themselves behind a presidential candidate who they believe will deliver them from the rising tide of conservatism. After the election, they go back to whatever they were doing before. Other Democrats have involved themselves in single-issue politics—the environment, campaign finance, the war in Iraq, and so on—but these battles have failed to build a political movement. Issues rise and fall depending on which interests are threatened and when. They can even divide Democrats, as each advocacy group scrambles after the same set of liberal donors and competes for the limited attention of the news media.

As a result, Democrats have been undisci-
plined, intimidated, or just plain silent. They have few
dedicated sources of money and almost no ground
troops. The religious left is disconnected from the
political struggle. One hears few liberal Democratic
phrases that are repeated with any regularity. In addi-
tion, there is no consistent Democratic world view or
ideology. Most congressional Democrats raise their
own money, do their own polls, and vote every which
way. Democrats have little or no clear identity except
by reference to what conservatives say about them.

Self-styled Democratic centrists, such as those
of the Democratic Leadership Council, attribute the
party's difficulties to a failure to respond to an electorate grown more conservative, upscale and suburban. This is nonsense. The biggest losses for
Democrats since 1980 have not been among suburban
voters but among America's giant middle and working
classes—especially white workers without four-year
college degrees, once part of the Democratic base.
Not incidentally, these are the same people who have
lost the most economic ground over the last quarter
century.

Democrats could have responded with bold
plans for jobs, schools, health care, and retirement
security. They could have delivered a strong message
about the responsibility of corporations to help their
employees in all these respects, and of wealthy elites
not to corrupt politics with money. In the wake of the
9/11 attack, the Democratic Party could have used the
threat of terrorism to inspire the same sort of sacrifice
and solidarity that it did in World War II—including

higher taxes on the wealthy to pay for what needs doing. In short, they could have turned themselves into a populist movement to take back democracy from increasingly concentrated wealth and power.

But Democrats did none of this. So radical conservatives eagerly stepped into the void, claiming the populist mantle and blaming liberal elites for what's gone wrong with America. The question ahead is whether Democrats can reclaim it.

The rush by many Democrats in recent years to the so-called center has been a pathetic substitute for talking candidly about what the nation needs to do and for fueling a movement based on liberal values. In truth, America has no consistent political center. Polls reflect little more than reflexive responses to what people have most recently heard about an issue. Meanwhile, the so-called center has continued to shift to the right because conservative Republicans stay put while Democrats keep meeting them halfway.

Democrats who eschew movement politics point to Bill Clinton's apparent success in repositioning the party in the center during the 1990s. Clinton was (and is) a remarkably gifted politician who accomplished something no Democrat since Franklin Delano Roosevelt had done: he got reelected. But his effect on the party was to blur rather than clarify what Democrats stand for. As a result, Clinton neither started nor sustained anything that might be called a political movement.

This handicapped his administration from the start. In 1994, when battling for his health-care proposal, Clinton had no broad-based political movement behind him. Even though polls showed support among a majority of Americans, it wasn't enough to overcome the conservative effort on the other side. But George W. Bush got his tax cuts through Congress, even though Americans were ambivalent about them. President Bush had a political movement behind him that supplied the muscle he needed.

In the months leading up to the 1996 election, Clinton famously triangulated—finding positions equidistant between the Democrat and the Republican—and ran for reelection on tiny issues like the V-chip and school uniforms. The strategy worked, but it was a Pyrrhic victory. Had Clinton told Americans the truth—that when the economic boom went bust we'd have to face the challenges of a country that was concentrating more wealth and power in fewer hands—he could have built a long-term mandate for change. By the late '90s the nation finally had the wherewithal to expand prosperity by investing in people, especially their education and health. But because Clinton was reelected without any mandate, the nation was confused about what needed to be accomplished and easily distracted by conservative fulminations against a president who lied about sex.

In future years, Democrats should pay close attention to what Republicans have learned about winning over the long run. First, it is crucial to build a political movement that will endure beyond particular electoral contests. Second, in order for a presidency to be effective, it needs a movement that mobilizes Americans behind it. Finally, any political movement derives its durability from the clarity of its convictions.

Progressive Blues

Michael C. Dawson

Rick Perlstein has a laudable goal—the crafting of a strategy that will ensure a lasting progressive electoral majority centered on the Democratic Party. While some might question the focus on the Democratic Party, the need to forge a new majority based on progressive principles and aggressive tactics cannot be doubted. Perlstein does an admirable job of diagnosing the problems facing the Democrats as well as suggesting some solutions. But Perlstein's approach is likely to fail because he has failed to directly address the century-old Achilles' heel of the left—the deep fissure of race which continues to undermine efforts to build a broad multiracial progressive coalition.

Perlstein is correct about many important points. First, as his analyses suggest, the great benefits that Boeing reaped when it focused on long-term investment and strategies (and, conversely, the catastrophe that occurred when it started focusing on short-term profits) provide an important lesson for the progressive movement. Progressives need to put aside short-term electoral strategies, as the conservative movement did, in favor of long-term gains. Perlstein correctly argues that a new strategy must also focus on historic core principles—particularly those of economic justice—that can unite a majority of Americans. He makes the much-needed point that progressives in general, and those who seek to transform the Democratic Party in particular, must be willing to take the fight directly to the opposition. All of the above, he correctly notes, require not only patience but a deep commitment to principle and the goal of identifying the Democratic Party with a core, central message. Progressives must be as persistent with their message and principles as were conservatives in their own dark days of the early 1960s.

But Perlstein does not confront one of the key vulnerabilities that he identifies. He offers no strategy for addressing the racial divide that slices through the Democrats' electoral coalition. As Perlstein writes, both Democratic and Republican Party strategists see the white voters' identification of the Democratic Party with African-Americans (a phenomenon well documented by several political scientists) as a critical liability. This is hardly a new problem: in the second half of the 19th century, Republican Party strategists also complained out loud that their party's perceived ties to blacks were costing them white votes (blacks of that time overwhelmingly supported the party of Lincoln). The Democrats of today, particularly those who are sympathetic to the analyses of the DLC, pursue the same strategy as 19th-century Republicans and several generations of (white) progressive organizers—distance the party from blacks while concentrating on non-racial issues. The most progressive of this family of strategies concentrates, as does Perlstein, on an agenda centered on economic justice.

The problem is particularly acute for today's Democratic Party. While African-Americans remain a small minority—and they are declining in size relative to other minority racial groups—their geographical concentration and massive allegiance to a progressive economic policy, foreign policy, and racial agenda make them a critical component of the Democrats' base. Without black voters, the Democrats would not be competitive in the South. In key battleground states such as Michigan and Missouri, black turnout, or the lack thereof, can mean the difference between a Democratic presidential nominee winning or losing. And blacks can be a key determinant when an electorate is closely divided, as is now the case. Pragmatically Democrats need to pursue strategies that encourage energetic black mobilization at the same time that they want to win substantial white support.

The way around this quandary, we are told, is to push a universal progressive program that deemphasizes racial issues. Since many African-Americans are among the most disadvantaged of Americans, such a program will be very beneficial to the race without incurring the racial animosity that flows from over-attention to identity issues. But why should this strategy work now when it has been largely a failure for over the past century? For most blacks, concern for racial issues are not a matter of identity politics but instead have at their core a concern for justice and fairness. The parties', not to mention the polity's, lack of attention to these issues has led to a deep and growing disillusionment about racial progress in the United States among African-Americans. In March of 2003, 79 percent of blacks believed that blacks would either not achieve racial equality in the United States during their lifetimes or not at all. Conversely, 67 percent of whites thought that blacks had either achieved racial equality or would do so soon. My work has shown that black racial disillusionment has led not only to a massive rejection of the Bush presidency (he has an 8-percent approval rating among blacks as this is being written) but also to a political agenda more conducive to black-nationalist than progressive organizing attempts.

Dr. King asked in 1967, "Where do we go from here?" At the time he also saw deepening distrust and hostility among the races taking root. And he also made the argument at that time that black anger and cries for black power were the result of white backlash and an insufficient commitment to racial justice, not the cause of white hostility. We should not be shy in admitting that such hostility is still alive and well. A recent article by the sociologist Doug Massey states that a large minority of whites (20 percent) would prefer to live in all-white neighborhoods and that a larger fraction (25 percent) prefer neighborhoods that do not have any black residents.

How do progressives avoid alienating white voters, skeptical at best of a political party too closely identified with blacks, without further alienating a black electorate that is increasingly disillusioned, and which could either withdraw from the electoral process or turn to a more nationalist agenda?

Perlstein provides part of the answer. Progressives in general and Democrats in particular must commit themselves to a course that may be difficult in the short run, but that is most likely to pay off in the long run. First, there should be a debate about what is the nature of a new progressive alliance. Certainly the core Democratic Party constituencies should be included, but new possibilities should also be energetically pursued. Such a coalition would include old labor but also new labor (which is often composed of racial and ethnic minorities, many of whom are immigrants). It would organize around the concerns of women and reach out to younger women who are seeing their reproductive choices not so slowly being narrowed as the result of an aggressive conservative agenda. It would reach out to the new immigrants of this century just as the Democratic Party reached out to immigrants a century ago. But progressives would also pursue a dialogue about race that would openly address the grievances of the past and present, debate which are legitimate, which can and cannot be repaired, and what role the state should have in compensating those who have been disadvantaged by racial subordination within the United States. The process will be painful for all involved. But without such a discussion, without building a party committed to justice on all fronts, the Democratic Party will be condemned to a future of occasional victories but continued weakness.

Good Government

Elaine Kamarck

In 2004, the Democratic Party lost a presidential race by only three points and by somewhere in the vicinity of 100,000 votes in Ohio to a war-time president. Democrats were hanging their heads and licking their wounds but the blue party is stronger than it was in the 1970s and 1980s at the presidential level.

And yet some Democrats like Rick Perlstein persist in seeing a weak and "hollowed out" party. In 1997 this weak and "hollowed out" party managed to survive the third impeachment of a sitting president in American history; in 1998 it managed to reverse the trend for incumbent presidents by picking up congressional seats; and, were it not for the intervention of the Supreme Court, this party would likely have taken the presidency again in 2000.

Weak? Hardly.

Perlstein, like others, persists in interpreting the Clinton era as an era of small, rightward tactics invented by a pretty unsavory fellow named Dick Morris. No wonder he misses the big successes of that era and the dominant themes that have transformed the party and will guide it into the future.

To illustrate those themes let me begin with two stories from the first term of the Clinton administration. In the midst of the health-care battles, the political scientist James Q. Wilson wrote a *Wall Street Journal* op-ed entitled "Mr. Clinton, Meet Mr. Gore." Wilson, an eminent scholar of government, made a simple point: to enact comprehensive health-care reform the country would have to believe that government could be trusted to get it right; it would have to believe that government had already been "reinvented." Instead the administration was moving simultaneously on health-care reform and "reinventing government," and, Wilson warned, the country was not likely to trust the government to reform health care when the government had not yet reformed itself.

The second story was told to many of us by President Clinton. During the health-care debates, he was working a rope line when an old woman came up to him, pressed his hands in hers, and said, "Mr. President, please don't let the government ruin my Medicare."

Both stories speak to the same reality. In the early 1990s Americans wanted the security and compassion associated with the New Deal but they did not trust the government to provide it. The Democratic Party had to prove itself competent to manage the apparatus of the government before the people would allow it to fulfill its historic mission of creating a secure safety net. To accomplish this the Clinton administration spent enormous amounts of political capital to pass two major deficit-reduction bills in 1993 and 1997. At the same time the administration's "reinventing government" efforts, led by Vice President Al Gore (and staffed by the author), helped create a reality within huge portions of the government that would allow them to do more with less.

Slowly and surely, public-opinion polls registered the approval of the voters. Initially, only 17 percent trusted the government to do the right thing; by 1997 that number had risen to 38 percent. Clinton and Gore had begun to make progress on the major policy conundrum of the late 20th century: how do you govern in an era in which people hate the government? What do you do when the public tells people in government, "Fix this now!," but then says, "Oh, and by the way, don't let the government do it!"

The massive deficit-reduction efforts of the Clinton years showed Democrats and the country two things. First of all, that long, low-term interest rates and strong economic growth could create more jobs than any government program ever dreamed of, and second, that a government that managed its money and resources wisely was a government worthy of being trusted with greater efforts such as preserving Social Security and Medicare.

Reinventing government and balancing budgets barely show up in public-opinion polls. But to read these polls literally is to misunderstand the presidency profoundly. The great tragedy of the Clinton Administration was not that the Democrats looked like the Republicans—anyone who remembers the showdown surrounding the government shutdown in 1995 and 1996 could not possibly think the differences between the two parties were minor. The great tragedy of the Clinton administration was that just when Clinton had begun to get Americans to trust the government again, just when he could have taken on the "superjumbo" issues of Social Security, Medicare and health care, he was involved in a scandal and an impeachment fight over an affair with an intern.

If the Rick Perlsteins of the world are confused about the meaning and future of the Democratic Party it is partly understandable. The second term of the Clinton administration was wasted because of a scandal that should not have happened and an impeachment that should not have happened either. Before Monica Lewinsky became a household name the second Clinton term—buoyed by shrinking deficits, a great economy, and a sense that this team could manage change—was supposed to be about entitlement reform. It never happened.

The reason to "reinvent government" and work toward balanced budgets was not to follow the advice of one or more political consultants. The reason to do these things was to have the trust and the financial wherewithal to repair and strengthen the social safety net—the most important and most enduring legacy of the Democratic Party. That Clinton missed this opportunity for a dalliance with a young woman is something that he has to live with, but it does not mean that the Democratic Party has lost its soul, or that it is bereft of big ideas.

The social safety net—the Democratic Party's legacy to America—is more important in a global information age than it was even in the industrial age. But it is fraying badly. The fiscal crisis is real, and four years of reckless spending and irresponsible tax cutting by the Bush Administration have made it fray even more badly and have weakened our nation's ability to cope with it. John Kerry was talking about the fiscal mess the Bush administration has created. Perlstein's own data show that this is way down on people's list of priorities. So why bother? Because preserving and expanding the great social legacy of the Democratic Party in the 21st century requires a citizenry that will trust the government to do it and a fiscal policy that will give the government the wherewithal to do it. This may or may not be good politics. But it is most decidedly good government.

A Flexible Plan

Richard Delgado

Rick Perlstein argues that the Democrats have turned away from cultivating long-term values and constituencies and toward a short-sighted focus on fickle swing voters. This strategy has hollowed out the party so that it is in danger of forgetting its longstanding commitment to reform liberalism in favor of embracing whatever clamorous interest groups happen to want at the moment.

Long-term party identification is certainly desirable, especially if, as Perlstein says, it tends to deliver votes election after election. But one should take care that the faithful are being faithful for the right reason. Consider, for example, the southerner who continues to cleave to the Democratic Party because he longs for the days of such leaders as Orval Faubus and George Wallace and believes that if he sticks with the party, it will return to its senses and begin producing leaders like these again. Long-term loyalties are worth cultivating only if they are based on your actual beliefs, which in turn requires that you revisit those beliefs from time to time to make sure they are still yours.

At other times, your long-term beliefs may present a different problem. Conditions may have changed so that it is not easy to see what course of action a pet value dictates. Let's say you are a Democrat interested in economic equality. But what does that mean in an age of globalization? Job security for U.S. citizens and protection from outsourcing? Tariffs on imports? Deregulation? Bringing the minimum wage in India, China, and Mexico up to the U.S. standard?

So, long-term values are not always simply stated or applied. By the same token, the short-term pursuit of uncommitted voters is not always to be scorned. A group that is currently unaligned—say, Latinos, who vote Democratic at much lower rates than blacks—may, with a little realignment of attention paid to their issues (say, more to language rights and less to deportation body counts), turn into party loyalists, and for the right reasons. Just as many marriages start with short-term infatuation, today's swing voters may turn into tomorrow's staunch supporters.

So the line between short- and long-term loyalty turns out to be far from clear. The one has a way of morphing into the other, just as the two political parties have a way of trading places, with one now identified with isolationism and later with war; now with slavery, later with abolition; now with big government, later with the opposite. Despite this plasticity, Perlstein urges the Democrats to cultivate long-term loyalty and stop pursuing independent voters in hopes of winning the next election. He gives the example of Boeing, which rose to heights by dint of long-term planning and research, but today courts oblivion for pursuing the quick payoff.

But is a corporation the right model for the Democrats? In business, a single objective preponderates: making money. In politics, a party wants to succeed in at least two tasks: winning votes (which requires attention to short-run pragmatism) and running the country (which requires wisdom and the long view).

Perhaps a better analogy would be a diversified investment fund that invests some of your money in long-term stocks and some in more speculative instruments promising a quicker return. If, as I believe, a political party is more like an investment fund than like a corporation, Democrats should be paying attention both to their long-term values and constituencies and to the swing voters.

A final problem with long-term values is that they tend to be stated at such a high level of generality that it is not immediately clear what one should do to effectuate them. I edit a book series for a major academic press and read dozens of proposals from authors. Because we are looking for books with crossover potential, practically every would-be author solemnly declares that he or she will write simply, clearly, and for a mass audience of educated readers. But it turns out that it is far easier to say that one will write for a mass audience than to do so.

Similarly, saying you are in it for the long run is not the same as knowing what that means. One needs a plan. The Republicans had one: As Jean Stefancic and I showed in *No Mercy: How Conservative Think Tanks and Foundations Changed America's Social Agenda*, beginning around 1970 conservative Republicans deployed a series of shrewd moves, orchestrating one campaign after another with the aid of brains and money. They cultivated different constituencies for different campaigns and made clever use of the media. They funded a series of think tanks, each devoted to a small number of issues, and trained young talent for future leadership positions. They used resources wisely, concentrating on a few targets at a time—welfare and tort reform, immigration roll-backs, affirmative action, the culture wars, deregulation—marching on to the next when victory was assured in one.

This required "future orientation," a "long-term horizon," "thinking big," and willingness to dream—everything Perlstein urges upon his fellow Democrats. But it took more—the practical knowledge of how to make those dreams a reality, the flexibility to shift focus when necessary, the ability to size up and coalesce with new allies, and the willingness to work for 30 years to bring the goals to fruition. From time to time we all need to take stock of our basic values and friends. But the short and long term are intricately connected. Reminding oneself of a few core values is only the beginning of a much harder inquiry about what exactly follows from that.

Mobilize the Poor

Stanley Aronowitz

To Ralph Nader, MoveOn.org, and many political activists and observers, the remedy for the faltering Democrats seems obvious. Rick Perlstein identifies it as a return to a finely honed version of economic populism—finely honed because he seems to endorse Bill Clinton's second-term shift to fiscal responsibility (read balanced budgets achieved through cutting social programs, especially income support for the long-term unemployed, and slashing more than 200,000 federal jobs). Look at the polls: most Americans want universal health care and do not object to government programs directed toward fulfilling the long-deferred dream of increased equality. Perlstein's argument goes a step further to suggest that the Democrats abandon their incessant short-term strategies, especially pandering to the so-called swing voters, who are, in his view, not predominantly centrist.

The main problem is not the solution but the audience. Apart from its social liberalism—often uttered in a backhanded, embarrassed rhetoric—since the 1990s the Democrats have become a party of moderate conservatism, against the radical rightist Republicans whose national administration, following Ronald Reagan's playbook, has adopted a policy of military Keynesianism. In its pursuit of global dominance, the Bush administration has rolled up astounding deficits, chiefly for military spending; in the guise of Medicare reform, it has sponsored a massive giveaway to private pharmaceutical companies. The Democrats have consistently voted for these programs in great numbers even as they howl about the accumulated red ink. More to the point, after a stunning come-from-behind presidential primary victory, in spring 2004 a loyal Democratic Leadership Council member, John Kerry, could not find a surefooted way of addressing the disastrous Bush-Cheney-Rumsfeld Iraq policy, since he had been complicit in approving the Congressional resolution mandating the invasion. Nor was Kerry prepared with a bold job-creation program to deal with the growing structural unemployment in the economy. Instead, he followed a DLC-like course, promising tax cuts to corporations that did not outsource jobs abroad, and creating domestic jobs.

Can the Democrats return to their liberal traditions? Can they replicate the economic populism that animated William Jennings Bryan's three losing presidential races, which, with the help of the labor movement's 1930s upsurge and a terrified but visionary patrician president, contributed to fulfillment of the progressives' 30-year dream? I would not be so foolish as to predict that it is too late for the Democrats. After all, from Roosevelt to Kennedy they rode to victory on the basis of a solid, segregationist South. Then, in 1964, Lyndon Johnson capitulated to the black freedom movement's demands for an end to the legal basis of Jim Crow. This act of political suicide helped defeat the Democrats in all but a single presidential election for 18 years.

Yet unlike Bryan, whose rise was propelled by a vigorous agrarian populism, save for movements for sexual freedom, the post-1960s Democrats have not felt the heat from below. Owing to a national policy that favors big business, small farmers are virtually extinct, and the civil-rights movement suffers from very selective success. Affirmative action has swelled the ranks of black professionals, but few look back at the masses of urban blacks wallowing in poverty, especially the millions of black men who are permanently unemployed. The labor movement, which still accounts for 22 percent of the voters in national elections, is too scared and scarred to make significant demands. Instead it pours tens of millions of dollars into Democratic Party coffers and millions more into attack ads that help the party during election campaigns. In April 2004 the leading feminist organizations were able to turn out a million marchers for abortion rights, many of them young, independent voters. Kerry greeted the march with his usual "I'm personally opposed to abortion but...," and, in the same month, he went out of his way to announce his opposition to gay marriage. Kerry and the Democrats were constantly looking over their shoulders to the ghost of social conservatism.

Kerry never heeded the warnings that unless he opposed the administration's militarism and moved toward an aggressive economic populism that promised universal health care and real jobs, he risked defeat. Conservatism, as Perlstein points out, cannot mobilize the discontented. To be sure, Bush lost some conservative voters because of his profligacy. But to sacrifice the chance of bringing millions of new voters into the electorate for ephemeral conservative gains corresponds to the deep-seated reserve of the centrist strategists who run Democratic campaigns. The trick is to hold on to the centrists who, after all, have no place to go, while reaching out to Americans (perhaps a majority) who have serious doubts about U.S. foreign policy and are feeling the cold wind of economic insecurity, whether they have a job or not. For the new feature of the current malaise is that the growing army of knowledge workers, as well as industrial and service workers, know they are subject to outsourcing, technological displacement, and wage stagnation. Some may have voted for Democrats out of sheer frustration. Hearing no answers, others stayed at home.

Then there are the 20 million full-time workers who earn wages at or below the ridiculously low poverty line. The tacit policy of both political parties has been to ignore this large segment of the adult population. Some are immigrants who cannot vote. But most are eligible to register. If only 20 percent of this group—largely black and Latino—had been mobilized and actually voted, the Democrats would have won handily in November. But the Democrats would have had to acquire in platform and rhetoric a class line. And herein lies a conundrum. The 2004 Democratic Party was committed to a swing-voter strategy that implied a distinctly corporate and upper-middle-class constituency. Unless the Democrats seriously try to attract the largely unorganized working poor in the future, they are doomed to fight within the narrow compass of the fraction of the adult population whose economic station is toward the top of the social structure. And that is not the stuff that dreams are made of.

The Winds of Change

Philip Klinkner

I agree with Rick Perlstein that the Democrats should emphasize a message of economic populism. I am not sure that such a strategy is as beneficial as Perlstein suggests, but that does not matter to me. Economic populism is morally right regardless of whether it gains votes.

I do, however, disagree with Perlstein about his analysis of the Democratic Party's current state and future prospects. The concept of party identification underpins Perlstein's analysis, since party ID "is the most reliable predictor of whether someone will vote for a given candidate. It is a mighty store of value, party identity." Consequently, he cites recent declines in the Democratic advantage in party ID as evidence of the Democrats' current problems and sees expanding party ID as central to the Democrats' future prospects.

Unfortunately, there's no clear evidence of a significant decline in the Democrats' party ID in recent decades. According to Perlstein, Democratic identifiers have fallen from a high of 51 percent in 1977 to about 45 percent today. Thus, the Democrats have lost about 5 percentage points over the last 25 years. That's a decline, but hardly a major one.

Though they have not lost much ground in an absolute sense, Democrats have, as Perlstein points out, lost ground compared to the Republicans. This relative decline resulted largely because the percentage of Republican identifiers has increased by about 15 percentage points since the late 1970s. It therefore bears asking why the electorate has become more Republican in recent decades. Perlstein's analysis leads one to conclude that otherwise economically liberal voters shifted to the Republicans because they perceived the Democratic party as too wishy-washy or cravenly pragmatic.

But an analysis of the data tells a very different story. First, as Table 1 shows, the American public has become more conservative since the late 1970s. Second, as shown in Table 2, since that time, conservatives have shifted heavily toward the Republicans, more than offsetting Democratic gains among liberals. Thus, despite Perlstein's analysis, recent Republican gains have had little if anything to do with the

Table 1. Political Ideology, 1978–2002

	1978	2002	Change
Liberals	26%	27%	+1
Moderates	37	27	-10
Conservatives	37	45	+8

Source: Data compiled by the author from the National Election Study 1952–2002 Cumulative File.

Democrats abandoning their economic liberalism. Instead, the American public has become more conservative and those new conservatives were more likely to affiliate with the Republican Party.

Perlstein is right when he says that party identification, more than any other factor, influences how people vote, but this does not, as he implies, translate into any consistent electoral advantage. Indeed, the Republicans, despite their disadvantage in party identification over the last 50 years, have still managed to win a majority (seven out of 12) of the presidential elections in that period. Why is this? Not all party identifiers vote, and of those that do, not all of them vote for their party's candidates. Furthermore, though independent voters only make up about 10 percent of the electorate, that is more than enough to swing most elections. As a result, a strategy of winning elections by relying solely on the votes of one's partisans has never been enough for victory. To a greater or lesser

Table 2. Change in Party Identification by Ideology, 1978–2002

	Republicans	Independents	Democrats
All	+14	-7	-7
Liberals	+1	-8	+8
Moderates	+9	-7	-2
Conservatives	+21	-7	-14

Source: Data compiled by the author from the National Election Study 1952–2002 Cumulative File.

degree, any party that hopes to win an election will have to cater to the "stock-ticker rules" and "short-term whims" that Perlstein bemoans.

But even if Perlstein were right about party identification, I would still be skeptical about the utility of his proposal for Democrats to rethink themselves. Since George Washington ran for reelection in 1792, there have been 53 presidential elections. (I know that Perlstein doesn't focus just on winning presidential elections, but they are the most important and consequential elections for any party.) Twenty-nine of those elections involved incumbents running for reelection, of which the incumbent won 20, or 69 percent. The other 24 elections were open races with no incumbent, and in half of them, the party out of power won the election. In other words, if you take incumbents out of the picture, a party has a 50–50 shot at winning the next presidential election. I take this to mean that winning elections is a random sort of thing and not something that parties have much control over. Any sort of effort to rethink the Democratic Party and what it stands for is a rather futile proposition because events will outrun even the most perspicacious observers. Elections tend to turn on such unpredictable and uncontrollable events as wars, recessions, and scandals. Indeed, but for a semen-stained dress and confusing ballots in Palm Beach County, it would be the Republicans and not the Democrats who would be undergoing this bout of introspection, self-criticism, and self-flagellation.

Furthermore, if elections are hard to influence, party identification is even worse. As Perlstein mentions not once but twice in his article, party iden-tification is a stable and long-lasting aspect of social identity. As such, it is difficult if not impossible for a party to influence party identification absent some major event—such as the Great Depression, the Cold War, or the civil-rights movement—that causes voters to reassess their partisanship.

What's Wrong with Short-Term Thinking?

Larry M. Bartels

Rick Perlstein urges Democrats to set out resolutely on the path of Barry Goldwater, on the off chance that it will lead to the promised land of Franklin Roosevelt. I see three big problems with that game plan.

First, the idea that *any* policy platform concocted by pundits and public intellectuals can provide the blueprint for a "dominant political party" is far-fetched. Dominant parties are, as it happens, quite a rare thing in American political history. Since the 1830s there has been only one instance of a party winning three consecutive presidential elections by as much as ten percentage points. (That party was the Republicans in the 1920s.) FDR's New Deal coalition, which Perlstein takes as his model of what a dominant political party can be, was a product of voters' responses to New Deal policies in action—certainly not a prospective endorsement of anyone's long-term plan. (FDR ran on a balanced budget platform in 1932, precisely the sort of political trimming Perlstein is at pains to castigate in today's Democrats.) And Ronald Reagan was elected in 1980 in spite of the principled conservatism he inherited from Goldwater, not because of it.

Second, Perlstein's insistence that short-term popularity is detrimental to long-term political success is unsupported by any evidence that I can see. He notes that a list of ordinary people's most pressing concerns "reads like the score for an Old Democrat symphony": health care, earnings, education, economic inequality. So why are voters not singing along? In Perlstein's view, because solving those problems "simply takes a while in the conception, in the execution, and, not least, in the political promotion." But isn't that all the more reason to make a start, however small, on actual solutions?

Perlstein's prime example of counterproductive short-term thinking is Bill Clinton and Dick Morris's "triangulating" in the wake of Clinton's 1994 midterm rebuff. But he sidesteps the fact that Clinton's electoral problems in 1994 stemmed in significant part from exactly the sort of go-for-broke strategy that Perlstein himself seems to long for. Of course the political fallout was "not for proposing health care, but for losing on health care," as Perlstein puts it. But the fact that Clinton lost on health care is hardly unrelated to the fact that he insisted on proposing a reform package ambitious enough to cement Democratic loyalties for years to come—a package too ambitious even to make it to the floor of a Democratic Congress. That is what happens to jumbo dreams. In retrospect, how can any Democrat not wish that Clinton had been willing to settle for half a loaf? Or fail to see that doing so would have helped, not hurt, the party's long-term prospects? Or imagine that a principled defeat in 1996 would have left the party or the country any better off?

Third, Perlstein's notion that the Democratic Party "must give voters something to identify with" flies in the face of a good deal of evidence about trends in party identification, partisan attitudes, and voting behavior. Voting patterns have become increasingly partisan over the past two decades. At the presidential level, partisanship is a significantly better predictor of vote choice now than it has been at any point in the past half century. Nor is this simply a reflection of Republican inroads. In the 2000 presidential election, Democratic identifiers were more numerous than Republican identifiers and more loyal in their voting behavior.

Over the same period, partisan attitudes have become significantly stronger and more polarized. The proportion of ordinary citizens who see important differences between the two parties is at an all-time high, as is the proportion who correctly place the

Democrats to the left of the Republicans on an ideological scale. People are increasingly likely to like one party and dislike the other; and they have more to say about the parties' good and bad points than at any time since the 1960s. Perlstein's complaint that "it's hard to identify with a party when you don't know what it stands for" reflects a different political world from the one most Americans are living in today.

The *pattern* of open-ended comments about the parties' good and bad points also contradicts Perlstein's characterizations of the Republicans as a party of clear, principled long-term stands and the Democrats as "the party of...nothing at all." For example, in National Election Study surveys since 1992, people have had more things to say about the Democratic Party than about the Republican Party—and more *good* things to say about the Democratic Party than about the Republican Party. Moreover, the average number of good things people had to say about the Democratic Party increased by more than 20 percent during Bill Clinton's 8 years as president—precisely the period in which Perlstein sees Clinton, Morris, and the DLC diluting the Democratic brand.

Perlstein's more specific concern that the Democratic Party is in danger of losing its historical identity as the party of the working class seems especially odd in light of the continuing economic polarization of the two parties' supporting coalitions over the period he purports to be describing. Nolan McCarty and his colleagues have shown that the correlation between income and party identification has strengthened markedly over the past half century.

In the 1950s, Republican identifiers were almost as common in the bottom quintile of the income distribution as in the top quintile; but in recent years the top quintile has been more than twice as Republican as the bottom quintile. Put another way, between the 1950s and the 1990s, the Democrats' advantage over the Republicans in party identification declined by 13 percentage points in the upper third of the income distribution, by 19 percentage points in the middle third of the income distribution, and not at all in the bottom third of the income distribution. It should be obvious from this pattern that the erosion of the New Deal coalition over the past half century has little to do with the working class and much to do with defections among the middle and upper-middle classes. The problem is not the core but the periphery.

So what is to be done? For what it is worth, here is my game plan. First, win. Second, govern. Third, win again. Fourth, keep at it.

Perlstein Replies

Adolph Reed and Dan Cantor wonder about the sanity of those who disagree with my general orientation. Bill Galston, Ruy Teixeira, and Elaine Kamarck find my views so outlandish they don't know where to begin. Teixeira's Web site, "Donkey Rising," has been calling for a truce "between the centrists and progressive-populists in the Democratic Party" but it is clearly not yet time for the honeymoon. I welcome the opportunity to clarify the debate as I see it.

One general observation before proceeding: my sharpest critics, all relatively close to the centers of power in the Democratic Party, appear to share some satisfaction with the status quo: a tie. They seem to embrace a "median voter theorem" intuition, the idea that the safest way to win an election is with 50 percent-plus-one of the votes: count on your base, then nose yourself over the line by attracting voters in the center. But it is precisely my suspicion that the more times this game is repeated, the less safe it becomes, because the very ideological timidity it requires erodes the base. Thus my central contention: these are self defeating, *short term* strategies

Keep that in mind as I take up five issues raised in the responses.

Corporations and parties. Richard Delgado gives me a chance to clarify my business analogy. The kind of company that I use as a model operates on two levels, profit-making in the short term and institution-building in the long term, structured around a relatively organic set of core commitments. The two levels are mutually reinforcing. Likewise in a healthy political party: an organic core identity and a record of pragmatic electoral success should be mutually reinforcing. An investment fund has no core values; it can fold up shop, cash out its shareholders, and no one need mourn the loss. A political party, on the other hand, needs to nurture a minimal core identity in order to get people to identify with it. Nothing I say here should be read to contradict Bartels's Law—"First, win. Second, govern. Third, win again. Fourth, keep at it"—but there are better and worse ways of winning battles, and the best ways are the ones that help win wars. Thirty years' wars.

But Bartels goes astray in the thickets of intention. Yes, the programs that drove Democratic control from the 1930s through the 1960s—I am including the 1950s because Eisenhower oversaw a moderate expansion, not a retrenchment, of the New Deal agenda—were not the result of self-conscious intent. But once the commitments were made, they were institutionalized. So the description of this period as a relatively consistent multi-generational project, adding value by its very consistency, still stands. But consistency can also be planned. Any competent history of the Republicans will show how conservatives settled on a small set of core commitments since the 1970s and successfully pressured the party to stick to them. This clarity, I argue, allowed an agenda often unpopular in its particulars to carry many more elections than it should have. The Democrats should aim for clarity, too—not least because economic-populist proposals are popular; also not least because, as Klinkner notes, they are morally imperative.

Parties and strategies. Dan Cantor is a hero of mine, and one of these decades I would love to see him reflect about what his experience with the Working Families Party in New York has taught him about how the Democrats should run their presidential campaigns. I am glad to wait; he is doing crucial work in the interim.

Phil Klinkner is a marvelously ornery political thinker, but he takes the discussion of political strategy off course by belaboring the question of how many people call themselves "liberals." The best evidence I know shows that when most people are asked their position on "issues," they answer like economic populists. So it seems reasonable to me that they would be attracted to a party that champions economic populism. You don't have to call it "liberal." I don't care if you call it a ham sandwich.

Michael Dawson is right: I offer no strategy on race. May I propose a piece of such a strategy? Republicans understand the political juice that can be squeezed from white Americans' deep desire not to see themselves as racist. John F. Kennedy took brilliant advantage of an analogous dynamic by slyly prodding Nixon leaners into questioning whether anti-Catholic prejudice influenced their preference. Today's Democrats could work a similar trick by nominating an African-American vice presidential candidate and hinting, "We know you are not going to vote for the Republicans just because you don't want a black person a heartbeat away from the presidency."

The forces pushing the Democrats right. Of all these commentators, Adolph Reed is the one who pushes me the furthest. His attention to the political ecology of consultantland leads inevitably to a discussion of the political ecology of money. Consultants and money are both implicated in the Democrats' retreat from a politics of popular mobilization.

For example, one Democratic consultant has published focus-group findings describing voters' deep mistrust of multinational corporations. His firm's web site boasts that his company's research has "helped the CEO and top executives of a Fortune 100 multinational pull off three high profile mergers and acquisitions in just three years" and also "helped a Fortune 100 manufacturing company improve the alignment of its employees around/with its new corporate mission." I detect a conflict of interest. Is this consultant using the data he's gleaned on popular anti-corporate animus to serve his corporate clients? Would this consultant avoid giving Democratic candidates "Rage against Corporation X!" advice that might make it easier for them to get elected even if it conflicted with the interests of one of those clients?

I raise the point to help Bill Galston understand what goes on in the minds of those who conflate the DLC and Dick Morris as forces that have converged, objectively, on the conviction that the best way forward for the Democratic Party is to preserve the end of the age of big government. The dominant social reality of recent decades—future historians will judge our era strange for not questioning it more insistently—is increasing economic unfairness. Yet many establishment Democrats still deny a core lesson of history: that economic anxiety (of the sort Stanley Aronowitz and Robert Reich succinctly describe) can be a uniquely galvanizing electoral force. And the most elegant explanation for this denial is Adolph Reed's, and comes from Woodward and Bernstein: the establishment follows the money.

I reprove myself for expending too much energy in my essay avoiding what I call the *Bulworth* Tempation—after the Warren Beatty movie in which the presidential candidate uncovers the awful truth that the only thing keeping the Democratic Party from sweeping the nation is the Money Power, and is shot in the back for his dangerous knowledge. Blaming money for everything is so tempting because there's something to it. If you are trying to understand why so much mainstream Democratic strategizing makes so little sense, you cannot afford (if I can be permitted the word) to ignore its malign influence—malign because it operates at the expense of establishing a broader mass base.

Take "wired workers"—which the DLC defines as those who "frequently use computers that are part of a network and work together in teams." The formulation is conceptually meaningless (is this really a demographically significant group?), if not politically bankrupt. I have a loved one, a lifelong Republican, who fits the definition; she is a social worker whose employer has recently forced her "team" to complete interminable, infantilizing paperwork on networked computers, in order to better surveil them. She is just the kind of professional Ruy Teixeira's data has convinced me might vote for a party that spoke to her experience of proletarianization. Yet the DLC pollster Mark Penn (and Ruy Teixeira seems to agree) insists "outdated appeals to class grievances and attacks on corporate perfidy" would "only alienate" such voters. (The greater the salience of class differences in American life, paradoxically, the more outdated appeals to their salience are said to be.)

The idea that "wired workers" are somehow inherently anti-liberal makes no sense. So what accounts for this concept's introduction into Democratic councils? One reason, of course, is the aura of Third Way hipness it conveys. But *Bulworth* tempts me to suggest another: that the DLC had an investment, literally, in propagating it. The DLC may have pushed the idea so hard because it stood to gain financially from an association with the author of the "wired worker" concept: not a political scientist, not even a political consultant, but a California AT&T executive and DLC donor.

Bill Galston and Elaine Kamarck would serve their case better defending their ideas on their own merits rather than investing them in an attempt to defend the honor of the DLC. New Democrats were just eager, Galston says, to "spur the long-term resurgence of the Democratic Party." They had a funny way of showing it. After the 1994 elections Joel Kotkin, a senior fellow of the DLC's Progressive Policy Institute, called for New Democrats to cut Clinton loose in favor of a primary challenger in 1996 or even think about leaving the Democratic Party altogether. The DLC's Progressive Foundation put out feelers to begin a third-party movement—"a new approach," according to the PPI board chairman Michael Steinhardt, "to separate ourselves from the Democratic Party." (Whatever its self-mythologization, the DLC's relationship to Clinton was always exceedingly complex.)

The DLC does not deserve Galston and Kamarck's ministrations. But forget the DLC. Galston and Kamarck's points fare poorly on their own merits. Reinventing government is fine in the abstract; I am all for efficiency and competence (though I wouldn't bet an election on it; in a telling bit of pleading against interest, Kamarck acknowledges that such matters "barely show up in public-opinion polls"). The problem is playing into Republican propaganda. Because Medicare administration costs are radically lower than those in private medicine, James Q. Wilson's admonition that the country won't trust government to reform health care until it reforms itself strikes me more as ideological smoke screen than sound advice.

The past. My critics' historical recitals (and this includes Ruy Teixeira's) ring especially false. All stress Democratic incompetence in managing foreign policy and the economy in the 1970s, as if this were a live concern to voters now. They cannot seem to imagine how in George W. Bush's America the issue of incompetence—read a newspaper—might now break a bit differently. And what about Jimmy Carter's unrealized "promissory note" to evangelicals? In my reporting among evangelicals, many told me they embraced Ronald Reagan in the 1980s because he, like them, believed literally in the Book of Revelation. Winning without the South sounds like a wise course to me if the margin of difference must come from advocating the restoration of Solomon's Temple in Jerusalem. (Of course one way to win *with* the South might be by mobilizing black voters with a black vice-presidential candidate. See above.)

What my critics seem to want is to once more march a Democratic presidential candidate along an ideological path defined by Republicans, and then blame the candidate for not doing *enough* to rehabilitate the Democrats' image. Much centrist Democratic strategy works exactly this self-defeating way. Take the idea of deficit reduction as end-in-itself as a political platform. All that means is that conservatives have boxed Democrats into a corner where they cannot propose any new programs, no matter how sound or popular, because the proposal will be shredded by the Republicans as a budget buster.

The future. Where does hope lie for those who find this insane? My intuition is different from the sort of "open-source, collaborative politics" that Dan Carol imagines, a coral reef of a million self-activating coalitions. "Test marketing," Carol's other suggestion—the endless feedback loop of sampling, adjusting, then sampling again—is the Dick Morris model by another name.

What is the way forward for the Democrats? First we have to convince the people we have a fighting faith, too. Or else you can't fight.

Fortunately, we do have one: "that government can help provide us with the basic tools we need to live out the American dream."

Language like this would sound crazy—paleoliberal crazy—if this were not a direct quote from a recent speech from the only Democratic hero to emerge from the mess on November 2: Barack Obama. Amidst all the talk of Obama's shimmering appeal to a post-racial future, his light touch on the stump, his language of faith and family and responsibility—all the things that convinced centrists he was fundamentally one of them—what most commentators managed to ignore was that the core of Obama's campaign was traditional economic liberalism.

He delivered that message up and down the state of Illinois, even in its "conservative" southern portions. Rather like in an earlier Illinois senate race. In the second Lincoln-Douglas debate, Stephen Douglas said his opponent would be singing a different, conservative tune once he was "trotted down into Egypt"—using the nickname that signified downstate's

fundamental cultural affinity to the slaveholding
South. Lincoln, like Barack, did no such thing: he
pulled no punches on his core economic message—
anywhere. The difference is that Obama won where
Lincoln lost. Obama has a winning message, whose
time is ripe: that government can help people overcome their economic vulnerability. That message
Kerry was not able to forthrightly deliver. It is a major
reason he lost.

This is not to slight Obama's extraordinary
skill in framing his liberal convictions on economics in
ways that offended few cultural sensibilities. He did it,
however, while never splitting the difference with the
Republicans programatically. Obama understood that
policies that close the inequality gap, in a time of
economic vulnerability, are a punch to the gut of a
conservative coalition that is a lot more fragile than at
first it appears. It will take some time to get there. But
now is the time to begin. ■

Contributors

Rick Perlstein is the author of *Before the Storm: Barry Goldwater and the Unmaking of the American Consensus* and the former national political correspondent for the *Village Voice*.

Stanley Aronowitz is a distinguished professor of sociology and urban education at the CUNY Graduate Center. He is the author of 16 books, most recently *How Class Works*.

Larry M. Bartels directs the Center for the Study of Democratic Politics in Princeton University's Woodrow Wilson School of Public and International Affairs. He was a 2004 Carnegie Scholar.

Daniel Cantor is the executive director of the Working Families Party of New York.

Dan Carol is a Democratic political strategist and a founding partner of CTSG, a progressive consulting firm based in Eugene, Oregon, and Washington, D.C.

Michael C. Dawson is a professor of government and Afro-American studies at Harvard University.

Richard Delgado is the Derrick A. Bell Fellow and a professor of law at the University of Pittsburgh.

William A. Galston is the Saul Stern Professor at the University of Maryland School of Public Affairs and the director of the Institute for Philosophy and Public Policy. He was President Clinton's deputy assistant for domestic policy (1993–1995) and is the author of, most recently, *Liberal Pluralism*.

Elaine Kamarck is a professor at the John F. Kennedy School of Government at Harvard University. She was Vice President Al Gore's senior policy adviser.

Philip Klinkner is the James S. Sherman Associate Professor of Government at Hamilton College and the co-author of *The Unsteady March: The Rise and Decline of Racial Equality in America*.

Adolph Reed, Jr. is a professor of political science at the University of Pennsylvania and a member of the Interim National Council of the Labor Party.

Robert B. Reich is the Maurice Hexter Professor of Social and Economic Policy at Brandeis University and the author of *Reason*. He was the Secretary of Labor under President Clinton.

Ruy Teixeira is a senior fellow at The Century Foundation and the Center for American Progress. *The Emerging Democratic Majority*, co-authored with John Judis, has just been reissued in paperback.

Also available from Prickly Paradigm Press: